ACCLAIM FOR *UNDETERRED* FROM AROUND THE GLOBE

"After reading *Undeterred* by Rania Habiby Anderson, I felt a sense of not being alone, of not being 'mad,' as some people called me, of not being from another planet. Now I know, from reading about the research Rania conducted, that the actions I took to implement Strate, the electronic settlement for transactions in securities in South Africa, were based on the habits many successful women in emerging markets have been applying all along.

"The developed world was asking why I wanted to run before I could walk. I said, 'Why not?' By following these habits, I proved that magic can be created against all odds. Today, South African financial markets are categorized among the top financial markets. It was an attitude of acceleration that brought us success along with an immense desire to make a difference to South Africa so we could create a better future for all.

"This book will inspire you to go out there and make a difference without allowing others to put you down or prevent you from fulfilling your dream. I wish I had read this book many years ago so I did not have to feel like the tortoise running a race against the hare."

MONICA SINGER
CEO of Strate, South Africa

"This book will open your mind and heart to the many ways in which you can become more assertive when it comes to pursuing your entrepreneurial dreams and aspirations. Read it, reflect upon it, and implement its outstanding advice."

MAURO F. GUILLEN

Director, the Lauder Institute and the Wharton School, author of *Women Entrepreneurs: Inspiring Stories from Emerging Economies and Developing Countries*

"Finally, a book that looks at how women in Africa, Asia, Russia, Latin America, and the Middle East are succeeding at work! Rania Habiby Anderson's interviews with women at various stages of their careers in wildly different fields are inspiring. The six habits she details are essential to success and helping other women 'get ready,' 'get set,' and 'go.' I enjoyed the book and believe it serves as a positive view at a time when the victimization of women is being used for various purposes that are unrelated to empowerment. This book is about empowerment."

MUNA ABUSULAYMAN

Philanthropist and media personality, Saudi Arabia

"The distinct personality traits, leadership qualities, and habits of women in emerging economies uncovered by Rania Anderson in *Undeterred* will resonate well with all readers. This well-researched and inspiring book will serve as a beacon for aspiring women professionals willing to introspect and discover their true potential in a dynamic environment."

ROMA BALWANI
President, Group Communications, Sustainability, and Corporate Social Responsibility, Vedanta Group, India

"The new generation of entrepreneurial women is leading a wave of bold progress motivated by passion, talent, and a desire to create solutions for the challenges of our era. Their impact is everywhere; especially in emerging growth markets they are redefining economies. *Undeterred* has amazing stories of inspiration and holds an action plan for your success."

CHRISTOPHER M. SCHROEDER
Internet entrepreneur, venture investor, and author of *Startup Rising: The Entrepreneurial Revolution Remaking the Middle East*

"Well-known advice columnist Abigail Van Buren once said, 'If we could sell our experiences for what they cost us, we'd all be millionaires.' But since we can't, we can do something else to make sure we profit from our own experience and that of other professional women: read Rania Anderson's fantastic new book *Undeterred* in which she provides a roadmap filled with practical lessons learned from successful women in growth economies. These women face many challenges, and instead of focusing on the obstacles find strategies and solutions to advance themselves and others around them.

"Ms. Anderson has done an admirable job of interviewing hundreds of successful women in growth economies and capturing the attitudes and actions that allow them to rise above their challenges. She has translated these findings into pragmatic steps that any woman can take to succeed. This book is a must-read for every woman in a growth economy!"

K. SHELLY PORGES
Former Senior Advisor, Global Entrepreneurship Program, U.S. Department of State, serial entrepreneur, and investor

UNDETERRED

The Six Success Habits of Women in Emerging Economies

RANIA HABIBY ANDERSON

The Way Women Work Press

The Way Women Work Press books are available at special discounts when purchased in bulk for premiums and sales promotions as well as for fund-raising or educational use. Special editions or book excerpts can also be created to specification. For details, contact orders@thewaywomenwork.com.

The Way Women Work Press
www.thewaywomenwork.com
www.undeterredwomen.com

Cover design: Carter Schwarberg
Interior design: Andrew Pautler, Pautler Design
Author photo: Jenny Wheat, Wheat Photography

978-0-9909063-0-8 (paperback)
978-0-9909063-1-5 (ebook)

Library of Congress Control Number: 2014954150

To the next generation of women
in whom I believe so strongly,
and to my father who showed me
the power of believing in someone.

CONTENTS

— GET READY —

— GET SET —

CONTENTS

— GO —

FOREWORD

Principal Investment Officer, Early Stage Equity Group,
Multilateral Investment Fund/Inter-American Development Bank

W HEN RANIA ANDERSON INVITED ME TO WRITE
the foreword to this fine work, I was happy to accept on
behalf of the Multilateral Investment Fund (MIF), which has
been helping women reach their economic potential for many
years. I'm also delighted for the chance to highlight the great
work Rania does through her organization, The Way Women
Work. Like her, I am passionate about seeing women succeed
in the workplace. *Undeterred* offers much-needed advice to
educated women in emerging economies who are trying to
advance their careers without leaving their personal lives behind.

There are no insurmountable obstacles preventing women in
Latin America and other emerging economies from starting their
own businesses. Actually, with mid-sized to larger companies

often reluctant to hire qualified women for any number of poorly premised reasons, small business would seem like a natural launching point for the more enterprising among us. So then, why aren't more women succeeding as entrepreneurs and transitioning career women?

In some countries, women seeking to start their own businesses or work in corporations face deep-seated cultural obstacles, including a perception of women's role being *exclusively* at home and the erroneous prejudice that women cannot negotiate as well as men or cannot excel in certain sectors because our brains are not conditioned for highly analytical careers.

Even in the more advanced emerging countries, men sometimes do not accept how women do business. Yes, we conduct businesses in different ways than men, but our ways are not bad, they're just different. Businessmen who don't adjust to women's ways risk losing out to half the global population. As women are currently graduating from universities at higher rates than men, companies have to figure out how to bring them into the workforce. The future of these companies and the global economy is dependent on educated women succeeding at work.

When the MIF started to apply a gender lens to our activities in venture capital and entrepreneurial ecosystems, we realized that women in Latin America and the Caribbean were encountering different challenges than their male peers. First, they did not have inspiring, realistic role models. Second, their networks tended to consist of family and friends rather than professional colleagues, thus limiting the input they received on how to grow their businesses, make progress in their careers, and lead balanced lives. Third, they lacked a roster of qualified mentors to consult when they were faced with professional and personal choices that affected their businesses. Fourth, as a consequence of the aforementioned challenges, it was harder for them to get funding to grow their companies in scale.

In *Undeterred*, Rania does a thorough job of showing the many challenges faced by the women she interviewed over the past four years, and of describing obstacles she herself has run into during her own thirty-plus years of experience. Instead of dwelling on difficulties, she highlights how she and the others overcame them with an undeterred positive attitude. She encourages you, the reader, to avoid adopting a doomsday attitude and instead to move forward by assessing the challenges and confronting them one by one. Written in an engaging style, her book features the stories of real women from different places and in different stages of their lives and careers who are true examples of focus, perseverance, and passion.

Undeterred is timely. Throughout emerging economies, ecosystems for entrepreneurs are forming. There is a renewed awareness of the importance of women in society and in the economy. In their homes and places of work, women are seen as essential contributors. Young women are pouring out of high school and college eager to start businesses. For them, the old dilemma of home versus work is something of the past, a lingering cliché. But although they have many opportunities, they also still face many challenges. I'm particularly impressed by

Rania's discussion of the gap between the academic knowledge of female graduates, which can be at a high level, and their workplace skills, which are usually low at first. Universities have to do better.

In any event, young women graduating from school or college are about to make decisions that will have lasting repercussions in their lives and in their communities. This book will help you build a better society where all voices are heard and all approaches to problems are welcome. It will be extremely helpful and inspirational, an excellent traveling companion for aspiring young women who intend to be undeterred on their paths to excellence.

I am grateful to Rania for her hard work and dedication. I confess to being a little skeptical at first that this book would be just another how-to book. When I started reading it on a long night flight to South America, I couldn't put it down. I read it cover to cover, so immersed was I in this book. I felt that Rania was personally challenging me. Her writing has inspired me to stretch outside my comfort zone once again. This, I think, is the best compliment I could pay to her and her book, *Undeterred*.

UNDETERRED

INTRODUCTION

"Without the full contribution of women,
no economy will reach its full potential."
Lael Brainard
Member of the U.S. Federal Reserve's Board of Governors

THERE HAS NEVER BEEN A BETTER TIME TO BE YOU! As an ambitious, educated, working-age woman in a developing or emerging economy, *this* is the window of opportunity for you to take *your* place in the rising global economy.

ORIGINS OF THIS BOOK

My place in the global economy has been slowly revealed to me. For most of my life, I wondered why I was privileged to enjoy so many opportunities when other women in developing countries were not. Early on, when I came to the United States from the Middle East to attend college and graduate school, I didn't know the answer. I still didn't know it when I was given the opportunity to recruit management trainees and then to develop business leaders at Bank of America. I got my first clues as I coached unemployed women during my first in-depth volunteer engagement to become gainfully employed.

The pieces continued to fall in place when I found myself increasingly drawn to help businesswomen develop, and to mentor young women. I got so much joy and satisfaction from my work that it didn't seem like work! Then, as I focused my efforts more intently in the region of the world that I had grown up in, the answer became even clearer to me. Finally I knew that I'd had the educational and career opportunities I'd had so that I could share them with you and other women. Today, I know exactly what I was preparing for.

Writing this book and putting it into your hands has been my primary focus for the past four years. Growing up, I was constantly told by my parents to read a book. I've always had my head in a book and I still do. I love reading and learn something every day from what I read. Therefore it was completely natural for me to see a book as one of the ways I could best reach you and as a vehicle to achieve what I now recognize as my professional purpose: to accelerate the career success of women in emerging economies.

THIS IS YOUR TIME

Throughout history, there have been periods of time that were particularly advantageous for specific groups of people. If you are a woman of working age in a growth economy, this is your time! You are in the right place at the right time to capitalize on unprecedented opportunities for women. You have the education, talent, and desire to effect change for yourself, your family, your community, and the world—and you live in a country where it is now possible for you to do so.

You are in this unique position because developing and emerging countries are still building their economic infrastructure and business ecosystems. Markets and businesses in these countries are rapidly expanding, thus creating new jobs. There is a need to hire and develop more talented people with the specific knowledge and skills to fill all the new positions. In this book, I refer to these developing and emerging markets as *growth economies*. As a woman in a growth economy today you can expect greater career and business opportunities than women in your country have ever had before.

The number of opportunities for educated women in growth economies will soon equal the number of opportunities available to men. In fact, soon women with university degrees and certain types of expertise won't necessarily have to compete with men for jobs at all. As José Ángel Gurría, Secretary-General of the Organisation for Economic Cooperation and Development, asserts, "Women are the most underutilized asset in the world's economy."[1] This is also the time for women in the growth economies to excel because their countries are waking up to the value of their skills and insights, and to the need for gender equality.

Four forces are working together to create this extraordinary and unprecedented time for you.

1. *You have an education.* If you are a college graduate, you have a higher level of education than many women in your country have ever had.

2. *You are needed.* Companies, markets, your country, and the world economy have a significant need for entrepreneurs with education, skills, talents, and motivation.

3. *You have new opportunities.* Growth, technology, and innovation are disrupting traditional business models and people everywhere are rejecting the status quo. These disruptions are creating many opportunities for you to act on.

4. *You believe in yourself.* The most powerful force of all is your belief in your own capabilities. Women today can participate at any level of business. We also know that we can have both careers and full home lives if we want them. We can design our careers and our lifestyles in the ways that makes us feel the most fulfilled.

As a woman from a growth economy and as a businesswoman who has seen and taken advantage of unique market opportunities, I want women in growth economies to recognize that now is the crucial time to step up and push forward into new areas of business. In researching and writing this book, I was driven at my core to equip you to excel as the new business leaders of your economies.

I WROTE *UNDETERRED* FOR YOU

Women in growth economies regularly tell me that they are frustrated that the vast majority of career advice available to them is written by Westerners for Westerners. They say that in order to get the help they need with their careers or businesses they have to physically meet with mentors or attend conferences and training programs. While such activities can be extremely valuable, they also require time and resources. Guided by my passions, beliefs, experience, and professional expertise, I am providing businesswomen in growth economies with a meaningful alternative: a culturally relevant "how to succeed" career book they could read and refer to whenever they needed.

I don't know about you, but personally I've had enough of the talk about the difficulties and obstructions in the way of women's progress. I want to change the focus from what is wrong for women to what is right for women, from what's standing in women's way to how women are standing up with new solutions for themselves, from the obstacles women face to the pathways women have found, and from why there hasn't yet been more progress for women to examining the progress that women have made. It is far more valuable to you if I share with you how women in growth economies are already succeeding, and the best practices they have used to get there along with my own expertise so you can achieve your own success.

MY STORY

I am a global citizen. My Christian-Arab family of modest means fled from Haifa to Lebanon in 1947, and I was born in Jordan in 1960. My father worked in the aviation industry. Because of his work, my family lived in London, the Middle East, and Asia, and we traveled the world. My early education included attendance at British and American schools, instruction in the Arabic language, and exposure to rich cultural diversity. My parents, brother, sister, and I spoke Arabic, English, and even a little French in our home.

Like most of us, a few pivotal moments in my life have influenced both my identity and the direction of my career. One moment from my teenage years set the stage for my future work. Growing up, my sister didn't like domestic chores such as cooking, cleaning, straightening up, and so on. She would regularly joke that she wanted to marry the general manager of a luxury hotel so she could live in the hotel and not have to do any housework. Our family and friends would laugh and say that would be a good idea for her. But I always wondered why no one ever said, "Why don't *you* become a hotel general manager?"

Interestingly, my sister pursued and has a successful career in university administration. She now works in Doha, Qatar, and is married to a wonderful man who is actually a whole lot better at household tasks than she is!

My own professional experience started in the financial sector with Bank of America and its predecessors. I enjoyed sixteen great years at the bank, during which I primarily developed managers and leaders. After achieving a senior role, I left the corporate world in 1997 and built an executive business coaching and consulting practice. I have been coaching business leaders, especially women, around the world ever since.

Throughout my career, I've been troubled by the following inequities:

- Why are some women given the opportunity to get graduate degrees, when others don't even have the opportunity to go to grade school?
- Why are some women encouraged to pursue their professional ambitions when other women are discouraged from pursuing a career?
- Why do some women have good fortune in their careers when other women all over the world face obstacles to achieving their professional goals?
- Why is it possible for some women to lead food businesses in the same regions where other women go hungry?
- How is it possible for some women to become CEOs in the same countries where there is also female genital mutilation?
- How is it possible for some women to work at the highest level of international trade in the same countries where women are being sexually trafficked?
- How is it possible for some women to hold senior

positions at utility companies when other women have no access to clean water and sanitation?

Four years ago, it became clear to me that I was supposed to use my knowledge about career advancement to teach women around the world. In 2010, I founded an online career advice platform, TheWayWomenWork.com, to specifically address the needs of women in growth economies. I was on a mission to discover and report on how women in these regions were succeeding, and to tap their expertise to help other women do the same.

I know that for women to take our rightful places at the global economic table, it will take much more than each of us managing a career and business of her own. Governments and businesses will need to make systemic and structural changes and are in the best positions to do so. However, often the best and fastest way to make a difference for ourselves is to first change our own thoughts and actions. When we change the way we view obstacles and the ways we think and act at work, we accelerate our own success.

MY RESEARCH

Experience has taught me that the best way to manage challenging tasks, goals, or environments is to observe, study, and emulate those who are already successful. I prefer to focus on people who are making progress, not on people who are stuck. This does not mean I ignore problems, or that you should. I want you to know that I am not discounting the depth and severity of the challenges women face. Here in *Undeterred*, I have consciously chosen to focus on what women do to succeed, not on how women are hindered from succeeding.

To write this book, I corresponded with, interviewed, and spoke with more than 250 women globally both individually and in groups. I compiled, analyzed, and drew upon existing in-depth research, information, statistics, and articles about businesswomen in the developing world. I wanted to find answers to two questions: How do some women succeed in countries where the working environment is not always welcoming or easy for women? Why are some women able to overcome hurdles that other women find insurmountable?

My approach to the subject was twofold: I decided I would go beyond the illusive "one-in-a-million," ultra-successful women that most journalists, writers, and researchers cover; the ones on all the lists of the "Most Successful Women" or "Most Powerful Women." I also did not want to base this book on the successes of western women because there are already plenty of books that take that approach.

I wanted you to have a book that represents women of all ages, each successful in her unique way, at various stages in her career and working in diverse industries. The variety of women represented generally typifies the different levels of professional aspirations that women have. I knew that I needed to talk with women whom you could identify with, be inspired by, and in whom you can see yourself.

YOU CANNOT BE WHAT YOU CANNOT SEE

When reporting on women in growth economies, the media chooses to focus primarily on women who are victims or live in poverty. What's missing from such coverage is the dramatic number of stories about successful women in growth economies, such as the ones you'll read about in this book. The scarcity of this type of information became even more evident when I searched in Google for how many businesswomen there are in emerging economies.

The search results returned me a question, "Did you mean: how many *businessmen* in emerging economies?"

Actually no, I didn't!

Undeterred contains the stories of women a lot like you—women from neighborhoods like yours and from families like yours, who work at all levels of corporations, run businesses, and work independently as consultants and freelancers. I connected with women from Abuja to Amman, from Bangalore to Beijing, from Beirut to Buenos Aires, from Cairo to Croatia, from Johannesburg to Jakarta, from Moscow to Mumbai, from Nairobi to New Delhi, from Saint Petersburg to Sofia, and from

Shanghai to Sao Paulo. I spoke with women who ranged in age from twenty-five to sixty-five years: entrepreneurs, architects, attorneys, corporate executives, journalists, scientists, doctors, small business owners, and technologists.

The interviewees, eighty-six of whom are featured in this book, opened up in unexpected ways. We laughed and sometimes cried. We almost always hugged at the end of our time together, having bonded over our shared experiences. I found that I never had enough time to hear the full richness of a woman's journey, and that I could have spent days with each of them. Their stories were real, deep, and powerful. Each woman told her story in her own way and took me through her life and professional journey, revealing the lessons she learned along the way. These lessons went beyond traditional career advice and management, touching on deep connections among family, life, culture, work, relationships, and spirituality.

There is no doubt in my mind that if you are looking for professional success, you will find the advice provided by this diverse group of women relevant, powerful, and instructive.

MY FINDINGS

I know that there is no singular formula for success, but through my research I have identified six powerful habits shared by women successfully working in growth economies. These success habits empower them to move past the obstacles they encounter, create a path where there is none, and consistently see the pathways, not the potholes.

> My research revealed that businesswomen and professional women successfully working in growth economies have six habits in common.

I found that if you want to work on your own terms, if you want a career—not just a job—or if you want to start your own businesses, you can. If you want to succeed, even if you don't know exactly where to start or what to do next, you can. If you aren't deterred by inevitable obstacles, if you are willing to try even if you are afraid, if you are willing to continue even after you fail (and you can expect to fail several times along the way), you can thrive.

Perhaps you are skeptical about how women in all growth economies can be covered in one book when every country in the world is different, even neighboring countries. In particular, you may be curious how I could account for the differences between women in regions on opposite sides of our planet.

Of course there are cultural, political, societal, and economic differences among businesswomen from different growth economies. I found, however, in my work, research, and travels, that there are universal truths and special conditions which unify women in growth economies.

In my coaching business, I practice an approach called *solutions-focused coaching*. What this means is that I focus my clients on specific, practical actions to get what they want. I don't spend my time or theirs digging too deeply into the origins of, and every reason behind why they are not succeeding. Just because you understand why a problem exists does not mean you can solve it. If you spend your time studying problems, you will only become adept at problem identification.

Often, the types of problems my clients and women in growth economies encounter cannot be "solved" by them. So my approach, and the approach of other solutions-focused coaches, is to identify and help clients take the actions that will get them around or through those obstacles.

I took that same approach as I spoke with women in growth economies. Because I believe that the most complex and entrenched problems are best solved by the repetition of simple actions, I challenged myself to find the actions that are working best for women and will also work for *you*.

THIS BOOK IS FOR YOU

If you have questions and self-doubt, you are not alone. If you are unsure about whether or not you can or should have a career along with everything else in your life, you are not alone.

- Do you have unrealized professional dreams inside of you?
- Are you ready for, and do you deserve, a promotion, but haven't gotten one?
- Are the odds of professional or business success stacked against you?
- Do you feel that your obstacles are insurmountable?
- Do your family and friends encourage you to stay home, get married, and raise children instead of working?
- Does your husband think it reflects badly on him that you are working?
- Do you think only western women have access to the best opportunities?

If you answered yes to any of the above questions, this book is for you. It will help you find a way to answer these questions in the context of your life. I hope you will take comfort in knowing that there are hundreds of millions of women around the world like you wondering the same things. Millions of women have found solutions and resolved these questions for themselves in different ways. I want you to know that the time is right for you to pursue any professional path you desire.

You are already successful. You have been blessed with so much. With your education alone, you are well on your way. If you are working, then you are even further ahead than so many others. For you, sustained success is now a matter of consistently executing these few key success habits and staying the course until you attain your ultimate goals.

IMPLEMENT WHAT YOU READ

HOW TO GET
THE MOST OUT
OF THIS BOOK

U NDETERRED IS DIVIDED INTO THREE PARTS: "Get Ready," "Get Set," and "Go." Within each part, you'll find chapters devoted to two of the six habits of undeterred women. As with all habits, these are comprised of specific actions that successful women consistently and repeatedly take year after year. These habits are connected and interrelated. As you read, you will see that many of the underlying behaviors of one habit are also part of the others.

To implement these success habits, please don't just read this book and set it aside. Reading about the mindsets and behavior of successful women working in growth economies won't make a difference for you if you don't put those ideas into action. To benefit from the examples and advice of these women, and from my expertise as a businesswoman, an executive coach, and a researcher originally from the developing world, you must also *apply* what you learn.

Furthermore, to build these habits and the behaviors and skills that underlie them, you have to do what these women do over and over again. Plan to read this book more than once.

Undeterred is a reference guide that will be valuable to you for many years to come. Reread sections or the whole book as your desires, needs, opportunities, and positions change. Each time you will be reminded of something you had forgotten, something you need to learn, and you will certainly find something new.

WAYS TO READ UNDETERRED

The best ways for you to read *Undeterred* are to:

Read to identify how you will take action. As you read, pinpoint specific behaviors that you can change or adopt and practice on a consistent basis—behaviors that you think will work especially well for you.

Read with a friend or colleague, or a group of friends and colleagues. As you read with your friends, explore ideas, talk through challenges in your country, and brainstorm solutions together. When you are reading together, encourage each woman to commit to the actions and habits she wants to adopt. This will increase the likelihood that you will each follow through on your intentions.

Read without judgment. If you read something you don't think will work for you or in your country, stay open a little longer and think about it further. If you read something you've heard before or already know, don't quickly skip over it. Pause, think it over again, and ask yourself: "Am I doing it? Am I doing it well, fully, repeatedly, and consistently? Is it a habit?" If I adopt one of the suggestions I read, would it enhance what I am already doing?

Take notes. Write in the margins, earmark the pages, and make notes in book or in the companion workbook (see "If You'd Like More" at the back of the book). Research shows that marking important passages accelerates learning. Note the things that stand out for you so you can incorporate them into your own habits.

Read to mentor. Think of a friend, someone in your network, a colleague, or a young woman in your community or workplace who would find this information helpful. Keep her in mind. Take notes for her. Think about how you will share the relevant parts (or the whole book) with her. Then take one more step: Set up a meeting with her to share what you have read in a way that allows her to adopt these behaviors and habits for herself.

The best way to read and learn from *Undeterred* is to regularly apply whatever you find relevant to you. As you do this, you'll propel yourself to success.

The women whose stories you are about to read are women like you. They are like you because they have the same dreams, ambitions, and fears. If they—women like you—are succeeding, so can you. But just like you, they have also had to learn to plow through their obstacles even though that's not what they were told.

As you read this book, picture yourself. Find the women you identify with the most. Latch on to these women and the ideas that speak to and inspire you. Do your best to imagine yourself taking similar steps, being resourceful in your own way. Most importantly, adopt the specific actions that you decide are most likely to lead you to what you want.

It is my deepest hope that in these pages you will find the inspiration and practical guidance you need to complete your own professional story. You can succeed even if you aren't sure exactly how to work toward your success. If you allow yourself to be undeterred by the obstacles, opportunities will open up for you. You are the woman the world has been waiting for!

Don't just stay on the sidelines. Don't just watch. Don't just read. Join us. We're waiting.

I'll meet you at the starting line.

UNDETERRED

READY

— HABIT 1 —

Be Undeterred

"Believe in yourself and all that you are. Know that there is something inside you that is greater than any obstacle."

Christian D. Larson

WOMEN THRIVING PROFESSIONALLY IN GROWTH economies have a common trait: They are *undeterred.* Undeterred women don't just go to work and survive the experience; they learn how to prosper and excel in their roles. They're not resigned to the problems they face; they thrive in spite of them. Undeterred women flourish where many women in the same circumstances fail to fulfill their professional promise.

Undeterred women do not allow challenges to stop them from pursuing their careers or business goals. They eliminate, reduce, or work around every obstacle that comes their way. Being undeterred means persevering despite impediments and setbacks, and being resolute about what you want. Of course, women successfully working in growth economies sometimes feel discouraged, which is only natural. But they don't give in, and they don't give up. The challenges of working in an economically developing country and dealing with gender biases may hinder them temporarily, but they don't stop women from pursuing their professional paths.

Women all over the world are told that workplace obstacles are insurmountable. They are led to believe that cultural and gender biases prevent success at work and at home. Rather than challenging these assumptions, some women decide not to enter the workforce. Others start working, but get discouraged when they encounter obstacles. Then they either get stuck or leave.

Undeterred women know that obstacles are a constant part of life; as soon as they overcome one difficulty, they run into another. What distinguishes these women and makes them worthy of our attention, is that they share courageous mindsets and have developed the habits that lead them to success.

ARE YOU UNDETERRED?

CLEAR
THE
OBSTACLES

CHAPTER 1

CLEAR

*"I don't see anything as an obstacle or barrier.
I only see the opportunity."*

Shahira Fahmy

Egyptian architect and business owner

BEING UNDETERRED MEANS BEING UNDAUNTED—
fearless—in pursuit of your goals, and not letting anything or anyone dissuade you. It means looking for pathways, not pitfalls. During four years of research, I heard the same refrain again and again in my conversations with undeterred women. When I probed into the challenges they faced, there was always a little frustration, even a bit of exasperation, as each woman would ask me a version of the same question. "Why do you keep asking me about obstacles?"

From there, the conversation would go like something like this.

Me: "Because I know you and other women in your country encounter many barriers."

She: "Yes, and so what? Don't you and all western women, too?"

Me: "Yes, of course."

She: "Then what's the big deal? Yes, we face barriers. Yes, we encounter both overt and hidden discrimination and biases. Yes, we work with some people who don't think women can or should succeed. But I don't think about and dwell on any of these things. I figure out ways to work around the obstacles that are in my way. Difficulties don't sidetrack me. I just keep moving forward. I always think about how I can make the best of any situation and get what I want. I know I can find a way to succeed in spite of the challenges."

The more women I heard make these remarks, the surer I was that success habits are rooted in powerful attitudes and action. To act in ways that lead to success, we must believe that we are capable of success. We must focus on ways to get things done. The undeterred women in my interviews impressed me with their unshakable confidence that they could find or invent solutions to their problems. This seemed especially notable considering the number and types of obstacles women in growth economies routinely face.

Challenges faced by women in growth economies range from overt legal and regulatory gender discrimination to conscious and unconscious gender bias. Many women also face a lack of social or familial support. I recognize that the types of challenges that educated women face are different than the challenges our illiterate and poorer sisters experience. Even though workplace discrimination is incomparable to lack of access to basic health care, water, sanitation, and food; infant mortality; war; and sexual trafficking—to name but a few staggering problems millions of women face—real challenges also exist for educated career women.

GENDER BIAS AGAINST WOMEN

Unfortunately, gender bias—whether it's deliberate or unconscious—still exists around the world in countries both with advanced and growing economies. You might be surprised if I shared stories about some of the demeaning and frustrating experiences some of my female colleagues and clients in the United States have had. You likely have had your own experiences or know women who have experienced negative gender bias.

As of 2013, 128 of 143 countries that were surveyed had at least one law on the books that discriminated between men and women. Persistent legal discrimination against women extends to activities like accessing institutions, owning or using property, building credit, getting a job, and starting a business.[1] Even in countries where common or civil laws have changed to be more egalitarian, customary law (traditional social practices) persists in discriminating against women. One example is the persistent practice in Saudi Arabia for women to have a male guardian to set up a business even though the laws were changed in April 2004.[2]

Gender-based pay inequities exist everywhere. Worldwide, women earn less than men for doing similar work. In addition, some countries have different retirement ages for men and women. For instance, in China the current compulsory retirement age for women holding civil service jobs is fifty, while men retire at sixty.[3] To be forced out of the workforce early makes Chinese women financially vulnerable.

Traveling to and from work has safety and financial implications for many women. I asked several women in Brazil and in India about personal safety concerns during their commutes. In Brazil, the women shrugged, as if to say, "Yes, that's a fact of life in Brazil," but also to indicate that they were not going to let the prospect of being mugged or harassed stop them. The women talked to me about having to be cautious and careful. I also learned that some of the wealthier women even have bulletproof cars. The Indian women spoke emotionally about their own and other women's experiences about being jostled, or what one woman called "Eve teased," and about the need to be especially careful on public transportation. The women have come up with and rely on several tactics to keep themselves safe. Women in Saudi Arabia face yet a different type of transportation challenge. Since they are not allowed to drive cars, getting to work can mean having to spend approximately 30 percent of their salary on hiring a driver.[4]

Obstacles weigh heavily into the decision of whether or not to work outside the home, where to work, how to get to work, and the hours that a woman works.

In Latin America, the increased number of female elected government officials has given women hope for the level of success that they can achieve. However, long-held views of women's roles on the domestic front, particularly related to child care, continue to limit women from attaining senior positions in corporations.

Around the world, especially in growth economies, women are expected to put their families first, for instance by taking care of their children and elderly family members. Flextime schedules are common in the western world, but less prevalent in workplaces in growth economies. These programs give women the latitude to come to work at times suitable to them, and may include working part of the time from home, making it easier for mothers to care for their children and daughters to care for their parents.

Even when women do make it to the very top of the largest corporations in the world, the expectations about women's roles prevail, as in this high profile case of Indra Nooyi, the CEO of PepsiCo. An article in *The Atlantic* reports: "I got a call about 9:30 in the night from the existing chairman and CEO at that time. He said, 'Indra, we're going to announce you as president and put you on the board of directors.' I was overwhelmed, because look at my background and where I came from—to be president of an iconic American company and to be on the board of directors, I thought something special had happened to me.

"So rather than stay and work until midnight which I normally would've done because I had so much work to do, I decided to go home and share the good news with my family. I got home about 10, got into the garage, and my mother was waiting at the top of the stairs. And I said, 'Mom, I've got great news for you.' She said, 'Let the news wait. Can you go out and get some milk?' I looked in the garage and it looked like my husband was home. I said, 'What time did he get home?' She said, '8 o'clock.' I said, 'Why didn't you ask him to buy the milk?' 'He's tired.' Okay. We have a couple of help at home, 'Why didn't you ask them to get the milk?' She said, 'I forgot.' She said, 'Just get the milk. We need it for the morning.' So like a dutiful daughter, I went out and got the milk and came back.

"I banged it on the counter and I said, 'I had great news for you. I've just been told that I'm going to be president on the board of directors. And all that you want me to do is go out and get the milk, what kind of a mom are you?' And she said to me, 'Let me explain something to you. You might be president of PepsiCo. You might be on the board of directors. But when you enter this house, you're the wife, you're the daughter, you're the daughter-in-law, you're the mother. You're all of that. Nobody else can take that place. So leave that damned crown in the garage. And don't bring it into the house. You know I've never seen that crown.'"[5]

Challenges are not reserved for women in corporate settings. Women who have their own businesses face a whole host of their own gender-related problems. About 80 percent of women-owned enterprises in India are in the service sector, but most bank lending focuses on the manufacturing sector. This puts women at a disadvantage. While male entrepreneurs get as much as 70 percent of their financing from formal lenders, this is not the case for their female counterparts.[6] Bank loans are typically secured with collateral; however, women in India, as in many other nations, often don't possess collateral because of the social, legal, and cultural restrictions on female inheritance and land ownership where they live. One of the greatest challenges female entrepreneurs around the world face is getting financing from loan officers and equity from investors.

South African business owner Tebogo Mashego candidly spoke with me about the bias she sees in the government awarding contracts to male-owned businesses. She runs a business that constructs gates and fences out of steel and aluminum. In addition to the gender bias, Tebogo's numerous difficulties have included having her business shut down by the police after neighbors complained about the noise and smell emanating from her plant. She has also faced challenges posed by the co-owner of her company, her husband, who has been known to withdraw money from the business accounts on occasion to cover his personal expenses.

GENDER STEREOTYPES

The combination of being young and being female can bring unique challenges. In many growth economies, recruiters and managers often refuse to hire young women because of concerns about how long they will stay on the job if they get married or have children. Michelle Wang, a marketing director from China, explained, "Many companies in my country hesitate to hire newly married women because they think that the women are likely to take maternal leave very soon and thereby create extra cost for the company." She was referring to the expenses of hiring replacement workers in addition to those of offering paid leave.

Twenty-something-year-old Polina Gushcha, CEO of Coface, a credit insurance company in Russia, shared that the greatest obstacle she has faced is the attitude of men about her age. "Frankly speaking, male businessmen, especially older ones, consider me to be not quite professional because of my rather young age. It is my task to ensure during our first meeting that the person I'm speaking with understands that my professional abilities are not age or gender dependent. Any age-related confusion disappears after the first working conversations."

A persistent gender stereotype about working mothers that a corporate woman, South African Tantaswa Fubu, head of HR for KPMG, one of the largest professional service (tax, audit, and advisory) companies in the world, still sees in the workplace is that "people assume that you cannot be sent on certain executive development programs because you will not want to be separated from your children—instead of asking you what your preference is."

Unmana Datta, an Indian woman and a former entrepreneur, who is now back in a corporate role, explained the loneliness that women entrepreneurs often face in her country. "It can be isolating, especially if you are running a tech startup. There are very few women tech entrepreneurs. When you look around at a startup event you barely see any. Then there's sexism and 'mansplaining,' which, of course, exists everywhere, from what I've read (and is probably no worse and even somewhat better in India than anywhere else). One man was always explaining to me that we were building our product on the wrong technology. My reaction was to think, *No, bro—I know a little about tech. I knew these guys' arguments were laughable.*" She continued, "Another man joked about who wears the pants in our house. His joke might have been more forgivable if it was less tired."

SEXUAL HARASSMENT

In addition to these types of challenges, women told me about the difficulties of working in cultures where men predominantly hold power and status. In these countries, business meetings often extend into the night and involve drinking at places where it is unacceptable for women to join in. Some conversations among men can make women feel uncomfortable. Men who may be working for a female boss or with a female colleague for the first time may resent working with a female cohort.

Power imbalances can lead to harassment. In one study from South Africa, 40 percent of the women surveyed reported harassment from men as a recurring problem.[7] When social power imbalances like this one are reflected in the workplace, they make it even harder for women to deal with incidences of sexual harassment from coworkers. Although the vast majority of women I spoke with only discussed incidences of harassment in general terms, one rising executive on the fast track in Brazil was brave enough to relate to me how harassment from her manager ultimately forced her to leave the job she loved and in which she excelled. After more than fifteen years of hard work and commitment to her company, which included relocating to a different city for an important assignment and numerous promotions, she reached the position she had worked toward. Tragically, her manager then began to make unwanted sexual advances toward her. Despite trying numerous ways to rebuff him, he would not stop and also threatened to use the power of his position against her. From her perspective, there was no way she could have brought charges against him and there was no avenue for her to report the situation. She felt she had no recourse other than to leave.

While gender bias is mostly negative and leads to discrimination, some women have positive experiences because of their gender. Being a woman is sometimes a non-issue, or in some settings, even an advantage.

SOMETIMES BEING A WOMAN IS A PLUS

Several women I spoke with told me that because male clients, vendors, funders, and leaders were sometimes curious about who they were and how they were able to get meetings or opportunities to make pitches that their male colleagues could not have. Some women also talked about the benefits they've derived from all the attention being paid lately to them through an increasing number of training and mentoring programs, and events for corporate women and entrepreneurs.

Neveen El Tahri, the first woman to own a seat on the Egyptian Stock Exchange, sometimes found her gender more of an advantage than a disadvantage. She told me that she was treated like a daughter and taught about being on the exchange by the older, more experienced men.

Indian entrepreneur Unmana Datta shared. "To be clear, lame guys were the exceptions. Most of the time, I met politeness and kindness, and was made to feel welcome. Some seasoned entrepreneurs and mentors offered time and advice, for which I am grateful. The flipside of being virtually the lone female entrepreneur, especially in the tech scene, is that you are noticed more. People are sometimes kinder to you and more eager to help than they would be if you were just another male entrepreneur. Organizations like Women's Web in India conduct women-only marketing workshops. Those are immense fun. Also on the plus side, I did meet a number of other women entrepreneurs, which is great."

During an interview with Argentine biochemistry professor-turned-entrepreneur Denise Abulafia, wide-eyed and smiling as she ate her lunch, told me, "I did my first round of investment *pregnant* with my third child. It was hard. My belly was huge and I worried that the funders might think I wouldn't be able to scale a business because I would quit working. However, they didn't. In fact, it was me who was worried." If anything, Denise was unconsciously biased against herself.

Denise and I met in the middle of the day in a part-brick, part-glass conference room looking out on the coworking space where her employees bustled about. She generously shared a local favorite dessert with me and went on, "It was exciting to find out that the investors didn't share my concerns. None even asked me what would happen after I had my baby. I raised my whole first round of funding in Argentina. I came back to work seven days after having my baby. It was easy, as babies only sleep and breastfeed."

CHALLENGES OF DOING BUSINESS IN GROWTH ECONOMIES

Often, the challenges women encounter in the workplace have more to do with how business is conducted in their countries than with gender. The same difficulties would be encountered by anyone doing business there. Both men and women in developing nations often face complex, unpredictable business environments, onerous and erratic regulations, inflation and unstable currencies, corruption, and cronyism. There are also other types of daily challenges, like heavy traffic, which produce long, unpredictable commute times in cities likes Sao Paulo, Moscow, and Beijing. In Cairo, Shahira Fahmy, founder of her own architectural firm, Shahira H. Fahmy Associates, which at the time of our interview employed more than thirty architects of both genders, told me, "I believe most of our business struggles occur because this is Egypt, not because I am a woman."

Yoanna Gouchtchina is a young mobile tech entrepreneur and founder of ZeeRabbit, an interactive social platform where brands communicate and interact with consumers. She finds Russia to be fairly tolerant of working women. Even so, she finds doing business in Russia to be very challenging, especially when it comes to working through local regulations and officials. She relayed how, in an earlier corporate position, she and her team lost a contract for a project they had been working on for a long time just because they refused to engage in bribery.

Similarly, Chinese journalist Zhen Trudy Wang's boss asked her to participate in a "red envelope" (*hongbao* in Chinese), a tip unofficially given to journalists.

In Argentina, I met with Maria Luisa Fulgueira, who has more than forty years of business experience and is now the CEO of Daltosur, a supplier of raw materials and chemicals for the cosmetics industry. Maria Luisa generously treated me to lunch at one of her favorite restaurants, an elegant place where everyone knew her name and warmly greeted her. Over lunch, with a good sense of humor, she matter-of-factly shared some of the complications she's faced in running her business. For example, there are restrictions on the dollar amount of daily imports she can make when ordering the supplies she needs to run her business. Daltosur has operations in six Latin American countries, with annual sales of US$85 million. These regulations would have killed her business if she didn't have the problem-solving approach and the determination of an undeterred woman.

PERSONAL CHALLENGES

Naturally, women around the world encounter personal challenges. In her exquisite art and furniture store, Badr Adduja, Jordanian small business owner May Khoury shared that she comes from a modest upbringing. As a young woman she won a scholarship to study at the American University of Beirut, but she could not afford to travel to and live in Lebanon. She married at nineteen and had three children. Tragically, she became a widow when she was forty-three. Moreover, her husband's prolonged illness had wiped out their financial assets. Out of necessity, the undeterred May figured out how to turn her passion for the arts and crafts of her heritage into a unique design business.

Alena Vladimirskaya, spoke loudly and passionately, as she waved her hands, about how she hit the lowest point in her life in her twenties. She was living out her dream, working as an intern at the Russian *Elle* magazine, where she someday wanted to be the editor. Then, when she was eight months pregnant, her husband left her. Not sure of where else to turn or what to do, but knowing that she needed all kinds of support to be successful as a single, working mother, she moved back to her small hometown and gave birth to her daughter. She began her career anew by setting up local radio stations.

The largest radio station in her town, which was owned by a well-known media company, noticed Alena's work. They brought her in to set up an Internet division in St. Petersburg. There she met and married her second husband, to whom she has now been married for over twenty-two years. Her career pivoted a few more times. She launched her own headhunting firm and today she is a tech entrepreneur. Reflecting upon the hardships she has encountered, Alena said, "Even if life knocks them down, women should not block their own vision. They should always move forward."

UNDETERRED WOMEN CLEAR OBSTACLES

When I sit on expert panels or give speeches, I am regularly asked what successful corporate or entrepreneurial women in growth economies are like. People often assume that undeterred women must come from a certain type of background, have a specific type of personality, talent, or level of intelligence, and have had to dramatically challenge the system they work in or the status quo of their cultures to get ahead. The fact of the matter, however, is that these perceptions are simply not the case. What women thriving in their careers in growth economies have in common are a set of habits integral to the way they work. The most indispensable of these is the willingness to go the extra mile and do whatever is necessary to find solutions to any number of challenges and obstacles.

Egyptian architect Shahira Fahmy, whose example demonstrates the way women look for solutions, said, "I don't see anything as an obstacle or barrier. I only see the opportunity. I don't remember the bad times, I think about the potential good times ahead."

Here's what the women you've been reading about and a few others did when faced with their challenges. After Yoanna Gouchtchina lost a potential client because she refused to practice bribery, she left her corporate job and formed her own business.

So she would not be asked to compromise her journalistic integrity, Zhen Trudy Wang went to work for a magazine that did not accept "red envelope" tips.

When Argentine shipping regulations impeded Maria Luisa Fulgeria from importing the volume of raw materials she needed, she told her purchasing department to place orders every single day for the maximum amount allowed.

In South Africa, manufacturing company owner Tebogo Mashego put in new financial controls and opened a different office so that she could separate herself (during business hours) and the company funds from her husband.

After the Brazilian woman who was sexually harassed reluctantly left the place she worked, she courageously and with great resolve started her own consulting business.

Undeterred women don't even let threats of groping or of rape prevent them from getting to their jobs. In fact, some women, like Indian urban planner Nithya Raman, are intent on solving these types of problems for every woman. Nithya has produced a plan to alter the layout of city streets where she lives and works. She explained, "I think there are two important biases among city planners and city managers that really prevent cities from being safer for women: First, city streets are planned and built for cars rather than for people. Second, there is a real bias against street vendors, who attract pedestrians. These two biases often lead to the creation of wide streets that are empty of pedestrians, which can be very unsafe for women."[8]

Sometimes women's husbands are the ones who come up with creative ways to help their wives overcome the unique challenges that working mothers around the world face. Indonesian entrepreneur Fikri Nauval, who owns a cargo and document shipping business, was inspired by his own working wife to add a service of motorbike couriers who pick up bottles of expressed milk from a woman's workplace and deliver the milk to her home where her infant is being cared for.[9]

In Jordan, Afnan Ali had to overcome many obstacles in developing TEPLO, a mobile personal heating device. The first issue was related to the type of hardware technology she needed, which did not exist in Jordan. She went to Germany and finally to China to outsource its production. The next obstacle she faced was to source investments for the hardware. She had to apply for prizes and enroll in competitions to secure the funds to start research and development.

Without apology, and expressing her steadfast determination, Afnan said, "I made a lot of mistakes and wasted time and money because I tried to build my product in the wrong ways."

Unmana Datta's unsuccessful business venture in India helped her to figure out a lot about herself. "In a job, you specialize at doing one thing well, or at most a few things. As an entrepreneur, you need to do so much more. This failure helped me figure out what I am good at and what I am not, and when I started looking for a job I looked for something that fit not only with my skills, but also with my personality. I am better if I have some structure, so I'm probably not a great fit for entrepreneurship."

A South African, Wendy Luhabe, who cofounded the first female-owned company to be listed on the Johannesburg Stock Exchange, Women Investment Portfolio Holdings, has led corporations, provided leadership on corporate boards, become a social entrepreneur and author, and received global recognition for her results and impact says, "The path to success for women lies squarely in their ability to take the road less traveled and to take risks along that journey. It doesn't matter if what a woman does works, or not. By its nature, the very act of stepping out in a new direction is already a contribution to the advancement of other women. Women have the responsibility to model a new way of being for other women. Just by virtue of their example, pioneers give other women permission to venture out and blaze another new path."

Undeterred women make discoveries while coming up with solutions for their hardships. In 2008, due to the impact of the global recession in India, Ritika Bajaj lost her corporate job. "I didn't know where to go next. I had never before had to struggle for work and jobs." Since she had already begun working on the side, helping an author with her book, she decided to pursue writing as a business. "The journey of the last three to four years as an entrepreneur and writer has by far been the most trying, as nothing has been certain. It has also been the most rewarding, as I have kept pushing myself outside my comfort zone, eventually seeing sides of me that I hadn't discovered earlier. I also realized I didn't need the security of a big organization. What I wanted to build, I could actually build as an individual."

Malaysian Wee Yen Lim, who has dealt with many types of obstacles in her life, exemplifies the undeterred woman. Her journey is a study in adaptation. In our interview, this young and determined entrepreneur talked about what she did to create a business model for Conspiracion Moda, an online designer clothing and accessory rental company. Wee Yen moved from Malaysia to Mexico and left the corporate world to become an entrepreneur. She did not speak Spanish, so she began to teach herself the language on the plane. Her Asian heritage influenced her to be humble and not outspoken, so she started by writing and sharing her business idea with various people in the fashion industry. In her previous job she worked primarily at her computer, but she quickly learned that to succeed as a business owner in Mexico she would need to adopt a different approach and adapt her work style.

She forced herself to get out and talk with experienced women entrepreneurs. She connected with several, including Celeste North, founder of NuFlick, a platform for on-demand indie films and film festivals focused on the Mexican and Latin American market, who became a mentor to her. Like all entrepreneurs, she didn't hear back from many of the people she contacted. Undeterred, she contacted other people.

Wee Yen's original business idea was for a fashion swap. That did not work in the Mexican culture, where women didn't like the idea of bringing in clothing and exchanging it for someone else's. As a result, she pivoted her business model to become a designer clothing rental business. When I asked her if she had any disappointments, she told me, "There's no need to die for one tree. There is a whole forest out there." When her Conspiracion Moda partnership did not work, she started a second company with the help of Wayra's, a startup accelerator, seed fund. This time she developed a shopping mobile app for Mexico fashion retail industry and fashion consumers.

How did these women become undeterred? Why did they believe that they could clear the obstacles they faced or find the solutions they needed? They took action. They started to make conscious choices. They deliberately made the same types of choices over and over and their actions become automatic behaviors. They developed success habits.

Women succeeding professionally in growth economies are not conscious of the fact that they are undeterred. They develop ingrained habits that allow them to figure out ways to accomplish what they want. Their success is not random. It is the result of their beliefs, desires, and repeated consistent action intersecting with opportunities.

Although undeterred women appreciate, contribute to, and take advantage of efforts to eliminate barriers like inequitable regulations and discrimination against women they are not waiting on the sidelines until they happen.

DEVELOP AN UNDETERRED MINDSET

What are your current mindset and work habits? Are you already an undeterred woman, like the women I've introduced to you? Or do you let societal norms, peer pressure, the business environment, and people's perceptions of you control you? Do you sometimes let the difficulties you encounter discourage you or dictate your life choices?

If you already believe that challenges don't have to stop you even though they may slow you down, then you are well on your way. Fantastic! You can skip ahead and start reading about the next five habits shared by undeterred women.

If you don't yet have an undeterred approach, you can develop one.

Even though the brain is not a muscle, it can be developed through regular exercise. Mental fitness routines are made up of our thoughts, our responses to the situations we encounter, and the actions we take on a daily basis. If we repeatedly take the right small steps, we can create big shifts in our perspectives, reactions, and environments. When you approach the barriers you encounter in a different way than you typically have in the past—meaning, if you begin to act differently—you will start to see situations differently and feel more confident. Instead of seeing problems as obstacles you cannot overcome you will find detours and solutions. Eventually, those same issues won't feel like obstacles, just nuisances you encounter in the course of doing business. When you to find a path forward for yourself, take it!

Start with action, not thought. Don't worry yet about what you think or feel, or how hard your circumstances might be. Your beliefs, feelings, and attitudes will be impacted by the visible and tangible actions you take. The outer changes taking place will begin to be reflected inside of you. We become what we repeatedly do.

To be undeterred, don't agonize over your problems. Clear hurdles. Look for solutions. Observe and learn from other women who have found solutions. I'm not saying to ignore the problems or challenges in your life or your business. I am encouraging you to take actions that change your view of problems. As you change your view, you will change your environment.

NOW IT'S YOUR TURN

After reading the preceding stories of undeterred women around the world, it is time for you to develop your own ways to clear obstacles. Here's how.

In the exercises below, I've developed a series of questions and specific behaviors for you to adopt. As you read further in the book, you'll see that every chapter has a similar reflection and action section. Work on these exercises on your own or with a friend, a mentor, or a group of women who are also focused on their careers. Take notes directly in the book or somewhere else, such as a notebook or journal, or on your computer. You may also go to TheWayWomenWork.com to get the companion workbook.

? SELF-REFLECTION: HOW CAN YOU BE UNDETERRED?

The two parts of being undeterred are:

- An undeterred mindset.
- Clearing obstacles.

Developing an undeterred mindset is about how you see obstacles and what you think about them. To assess your perception of the obstacles you face, ask yourself the following questions.

- What is my immediate professional or business goal? *Examples: Get a job, a promotion, a raise, or a business license. Start or grow a business. Make more money.*

- What main obstacle is presently in my way? *Examples: A person, a regulation, a particular bias, a financial need, or a lack of knowledge or confidence.*

- When faced with this type of obstacle, how do I usually react?
  Examples: Anger, frustration, immobilization, blame, giving up, or confrontation.

- On the rare occasions when I encounter this challenge, how do I work differently?
  Examples: I come up with alternatives. I work more creatively. I work with someone else.

- When I see others who overcome this challenge, what do I see them doing?
  Examples: They seek out alternatives. They are not bothered by the challenge. They find a way to turn the obstacle into an opportunity for themselves. They seek advice from knowledgeable people.

With your answers to the preceding questions in mind, decide what actions would best help you. Following are some ideas.

⟳ ACTIONS
→ TO CLEAR OBSTACLES

Train yourself to keep going when you encounter obstacles. If you don't stop, you will find or create solutions to reach your objectives. The key questions to ask yourself are:

- What one thing could I do to go around, overcome, or remove the obstacle I've identified?
- What can *I* change?

As you answer these questions, you'll discover that there are five primary ways to overcome obstacles.

Remove the obstacle. Based on what you know or from talking with others, is there a way you can eliminate the obstacle or convince someone else to change the system, policy, or procedure that's in your way? (Remember Wee Yen Lim in Malaysia.)

Find a workaround. What process or alternative way could you use to go around the obstacle? (Remember Maria Luisa Fulgeria in Argentina.)

Negotiate an exception. Ask if it would be possible for you to not to go by the rule or requirement that's getting in your way. Be sure to provide a reason for asking for this exception and the benefit of you taking the course of action.

Leave. Is there somewhere else you could work to avoid or minimize this obstacle? (Remember Zhen Wang in China.)

Do the opposite. It has been said, "Insanity is doing the same thing over and over again and expecting different results."

If something is not working, we cannot expect a different outcome from doing what we usually do. We have to do something different. The undeterred mindset is often best developed by using a technique I call *Do the Opposite*, in which you decide to try a different approach purposefully to see if you get a better result. In the table below are some specific "opposite" actions to get you started.

IF YOU USUALLY . . .	DO THE OPPOSITE:
Assume it isn't possible to overcome the obstacle	Envision yourself achieving what you want. *Ask yourself or someone you trust if there is a way to make the obstacle you're facing easier to deal with, even if it cannot be removed.*
Keep quiet about the obstacle	Talk about it with someone who can address it. *Depending on your situation, it may be most appropriate to talk with the person who has created the challenge or with your manager, a member of the human resources staff in your*

	company, a government official, or an organization focused on the issue.
Incessantly talk about the obstacle, expressing a great deal of frustration	Express your frustration through silence. *This approach may be particularly helpful during meetings or in a corporate setting, as your silence will likely feel uncomfortable to the person demonstrating the bias.*
Don't know enough about an issue or obstacle you are encountering	Learn more about it. *Research to learn where it comes from, how it started, and what those who created the obstacle are afraid of or guarding against.*
Stop when you encounter a particular obstacle	Go one additional step beyond where you would normally go. *If you typically only try once, then try twice. If you typically stop when you are told no, ask one more time.*

Avoid confrontation	Address the issue head on. *If you typically accept biases in your workplace, for instance, express your frustration verbally or in writing.*
Defer to the judgments of others	Clearly express your opinion. *Say, "Here's how I view the situation" or "Here's another way to think about this issue." Or ask, "Have you thought about the issue from this perspective?"*
Blame others or the system	Examine what you yourself could do differently. *Look at your own behavior and figure out one thing you can do differently to achieve your goals.*
Continually think about the problems you encounter	Think about a possible solution. *Reflect on ways you could minimize the challenge, or do your best to come up with an alternative.*

IT TAKES A WHOLE SET OF HABITS TO BECOME UNDETERRED

Thus far, you have read about the mindset and actions that comprise the key success habit of undeterred women. As you read on, you'll learn about five more habits that will enable you to professionally succeed on your own terms.

Habits are behaviors that are consistently repeated until they become routine, even automatic. Maintaining consistency with our good habits creates the positive outcomes we seek. As a business coach, I know that it takes a whole set of habits to achieve a significant result. This is the case for the undeterred women I met who are thriving in growth economies. They rely on all six habits described in this book to achieve professional success.

I know that maintaining good health and an optimal weight requires a whole set of good behaviors. These range from small habits, like regularly brushing your teeth and washing your hands, to big habits, like getting enough sleep, avoiding stress, eating healthy foods, and exercising regularly. I am consistent with all these habits except for the last. In fact, I am very inconsistent with exercise.

Some weeks I exercise four or five times a week, sometimes once or twice, and when I am very busy, I skip exercising all together for long periods of time. I can find a thousand and one reasons why I cannot exercise on any given day. The result? I am in generally good health, but I always carry around an extra four and a half kilos (ten pounds). I regularly talk about, and "wish," I could lose the extra weight. But talking about it and wishing it gone hasn't done anything for me. I am healthy, but not exactly where I want to be.

As I start exercising again after every period when I haven't been consistently exercising, I find that I am out of shape. It is harder for me to do what I did before, I tire easily, and the next day I feel sore. That tough experience causes me not to want to exercise again the next day, which is exactly the wrong decision. For me, exercising has never become a routine I follow instinctively and without thinking, like I brush my teeth, so I am not in the shape I want to be in.

Think about this analogy as you read more about the underlying behaviors of undeterred women in growth economies. Ask yourself honestly—do you engage in these same habits consistently and repeatedly? Or do you know about them and understand that you should do them, but only do them sporadically rather than regularly, like me with my exercise regimen? Are you "out of shape" in your efforts to achieve your professional goals?

It takes all six success habits, not one or two, or even three. You have to engage in all six regularly and consistently, to get to where you want to be.

SUMMARY

An undeterred mindset is the keystone of success for women in growth economies. To succeed, you don't have to eliminate all the obstacles or get everything right. Try changing your perspective about the obstacles and take actions that move you forward, around, or through them. Regularly looking for solutions has the power to transform everything for you.

Millions of women like you are figuring out how to get through and around obstacles. There is no doubt that you can, too! If you have been letting obstacles block your path it is now time to build an undeterred mindset by taking the repeated actions to establish the habits for your success.

The thoughts you think and the actions you take on a regular basis influence your brain. Over time, new responses and routines will override old patterns that formerly got in your way. Believing you can clear obstacles will change your responses to them and prevent them from stopping you.

The two most important questions to ask yourself are:

- Which of my typical responses to challenges and obstacles do I want to change?
- What specific actions or responses will I start taking from here forward to clear the obstacles I encounter?

— HABIT 2 —

Prepare

Preparation builds confidence,
courage, and competence.

ONE OF THE FIRST THINGS WOMEN IN GROWTH economies usually share with me is that lack of preparation has never been an option for them. A woman who wants a career or business in a growth economy simply won't succeed if she is *unprepared.*

Data from the International Labor Organization, a United Nations agency that tracks the global workforce, reveals two main reasons some women don't pursue work. They either are not prepared or don't have the resources or infrastructure they need to join the workforce.[1] Women thriving in their workplaces and succeeding in business have overcome these obstacles through consistent implementation of a powerful set of habits.

OPPORTUNITY + PREPARATION = ACHIEVEMENT

The foundation of success is preparation. The rest of the habits build on the habit of continually preparing. If you do not prepare for the successes and failures that are inevitable parts of doing business, you will have no way to attain the goals you set.

The great news is that you are already used to being prepared. Your preparations in other aspects of your life, such as attending a university or holding down different jobs, have helped you get here. If you make preparation a habit, you will build your confidence, courage, and competence. This is why undeterred women are lifelong learners.

Think of the habit of preparation as being similar to a pre-event training or rehearsal. In every competition or performance save one, participants practice their skills and train or rehearse regularly. The one exception is business. Although business is very competitive, many people think that they can win in the marketplace without repeatedly preparing and practicing their skills. But researchers in many studies have determined that skill mastery and expertise actually require *10,000 hours* of practice.[2]

Undeterred women in growth economies know that to compete and win professionally, they must be prepared. They work extremely hard to be as prepared as possible by developing the mindset, knowledge, skills, drive, and contacts they need to succeed. They prepare for difficult circumstances they know they will encounter, as well as for the opportunities they will create or find. They recognize that for them and women like them, the path to success cannot be left to chance. The way to success is too arduous, too full of obstacles and potholes, and too full of people who would prefer for them not to succeed.

There are two parts to the habit of preparation. First, prepare yourself on the inside. Then, ensure that you have the skills it takes to succeed. Both of these parts are needed to develop confidence, courage, and competence.

BELIEVE
IN
YOURSELF

CHAPTER 2

CONFIDENCE

"Success, it turns out, correlates just as closely with confidence as it does with competence."

Katty Kay and Claire Shipman

The Atlantic

J UST AS PREPARATION IS THE FOUNDATION OF success, confidence is the foundation of preparation. Without confidence, your habits will be as unsteady as a house built without a foundation. Without confidence, everything you do will be a struggle and you will constantly need external validation instead of feeling internally grounded, centered, and self-reliant.

Where does confidence come from? From action. More specifically, from giving yourself permission to take action while trusting that you are capable. It comes from letting go of negative judgment, rejecting discouraging words and thoughts from others, and preventing yourself from indulging in self-deprecating thinking. You will also feel more confident when you are prepared. So planning and practicing are crucial. You will also develop confidence by taking risks and experimenting.

Develop your confidence one step at a time. When you move out of situations where you feel comfortable into environments where you are less comfortable, or even entirely uncomfortable, you will gain more confidence. You will build your confidence when you trust yourself and believe that you are capable. When you make mistakes or fail, cultivate your confidence by being kind to yourself. Your confidence will grow as you push your limits.

During my research, women talked about self-confidence more than any other trait. They said that women in their countries often lack the self-assurance. *"Be confident"* is the advice they most often gave when I asked what tip they would like to share with other businesswomen. Here's what a few of them said.

- Michelle Wang, a marketing director in China: "People have heard many stories of career women succeeding in China today. A few sociological factors have contributed to this phenomenon: China's fast growth in the last few decades created a large labor demand; the one-child policy enabled families to provide sufficient resources for children to receive quality education; and an unbiased hiring policy helped women. If there is one thing that modern career women in China can do better to help themselves succeed, it is to have more confidence and be brave enough to experiment with new things."

- Manar Al-Moneef, M.D., Ph.D., COO, at General Electric in Saudi Arabia, who is a physician by training: "The greatest obstacles to a woman's success are within her. The key to success is self-confidence."
- Estefany Marte, General Manager of A.M. Frutas y Vegetales SRL, a fruit and vegetable business in the Dominican Republic: "For women in my country, there is the common problem of not believing in themselves. Latin American culture is male-dominated, but I think things are changing. Right now we have many female presidents in the region. Our vice president is a woman, too. But success comes when women are empowered from within. They have to understand they can do it. It doesn't matter if you give them money, tools, and training. If they don't believe in themselves, they aren't going to do anything with what they have been given. I am trying to work with women in my community. They have an amazing capacity, but often they don't think they can have their own businesses. I am trying to make them understand it is possible and they can do it. My dad started selling pineapples from his truck. I work with him now and we have grown our business. We love it, and I am proud of it. If I can do it, you can do it, too. If you are thinking, *She's rich, that's why she can do it*, or making other excuses for why you shouldn't try to succeed, you're wrong. It is not a matter of money. You can get there if you really want to! Whatever you want is possible, if you work for it."

- Small business owner and award-winning Jordanian artist, May Khoury: "Your success will be affected by the following: 1) the risks you take, 2) the opportunities you pursue, 3) the challenges you tackle, and 4) your confidence level. Success requires discipline, passion, inspiration, and high self-confidence."
- Violeta Noya, the no-nonsense, driven CEO of Otima, a street furniture concession company, in Sao Paulo: "I've always believed I can do everything. I always wanted to be successful. I trust myself."

Self-confidence comes from what you feel and think about your abilities. Of the many things that are tough for women all over the world, self-confidence is among the very toughest. But, many, many women all over the world are self-assured. Perhaps you are one of them. You'll meet some of them here. How did they get that way? They weren't born that way. They had to develop self-esteem and confidence.

Trust in our own abilities and potential to do well is not given to us, its source lies deep inside us and in the actions we repeatedly take. We have to go find the seed of it there—and nurture it to grow in our own lives.

EARLY INFLUENCES

We can trace our self-confidence back to the messages we received from those around us in our childhood and early lives, to how success and failure were viewed by our family (especially our fathers), friends, and other influential people in our lives. If we received positive messages about our abilities and desire to participate in business, then we were empowered to act. We could start to become familiar with professional work, which boosted our confidence. If, on the other hand, people around us doubted our abilities, we may have internalized the idea that we were not capable or that we had no right to want a career. Their negativity and the voice inside of us became a barrier to our accomplishment.

In most cases, the women I researched were very fortunate to have families that had more than just traditional aspirations for them. Many women trace the origin of their confidence to their father's support or influence.

Fathers influence their daughters in different ways. Talking at her second-floor office on a crowded street in Cairo, Egypt, Neveen El Tahri said that her father raised her and her two sisters as if they were three boys; he had the same expectations for them that he would have had for sons. As a result, from an early age, Neveen believed that she could do anything a boy or man could do. Neveen became the first woman to sit on the Egyptian Stock Exchange board of directors, a post she held from 1997 to 2003. She also sits on numerous public and private corporate boards. These are all the types of positions that very few women anywhere in the world hold.

For another Egyptian, Fatma Lotfy, the story was a little different. Seated at her large, imposing desk, Fatma recalled her childhood. There are four daughters in Fatma's family. Her father was a banker and financier and very much wanted to have a son. Fatma and her sisters were frustrated by their father's wishes and decided to prove to him that they were better than boys. Fatma and two of her sisters built their careers in banking. One sister is the CEO of an Islamic bank and Fatma is Deputy Chairman and Managing Director of Bank Audi, a bank with assets of over three billion U.S. dollars.[1]

Like these two Middle Eastern women, if I had to credit just one person with influencing my level of confidence it would be my father. The predominant perception of Middle Eastern fathers in much of the world is that they are controlling and are unlikely to encourage their daughters to pursue professional success. While that is the case for some girls in the Middle East, it was not the case for me.

When I was a child in the Middle East, my father worked six days a week from 7:30 AM until 1:30 PM or 2:00 PM. He came home, had lunch with my mom, and then both my parents were there to meet us when my sister and I got home from school. It was an ideal way to grow up, and I often reflect back on the benefits to my parents of having uninterrupted couple time in the middle of the day before either was too tired, as well as the unparalleled gift of having both my parents available to spend time with me when I arrived home from school.

Like many families, our family had a set routine. When my sister and I got home from school, we had a snack and recapped our day for our parents, and then we had to do our homework. I often came across problems that I could not solve. So I'd take my book, find my dad, and ask him to help me. It wasn't until many years later, as an adult, that I realized that my dad never really gave me any answers. He just asked me questions like "Where is the information about this? What other sources of information are there on this topic? Who else knows about it? How did the teacher explain it in class? What did she say was important? What specific part are you stuck on? Which parts do you know? What part don't you know?" Many years later, I realized that these are the questions I often asked myself in college and graduate school, that I ask myself every day at work, and that I ask my team when they have a problem.

My father's line of questioning nurtured in me the belief that I could find the answers and had the ability to solve problems. From him I understood that there weren't any problems I could not solve. My father's belief in me and my abilities gave me confidence to work hard to find solutions and to have the courage never to be deterred by the challenges that lay ahead.

One of the oldest, most tenured entrepreneurs I spoke with while doing my research for this book was Marta Harff, founder of a fragrance company that she franchised throughout Argentina. Her childhood experiences taught her that she had to rely on herself. During our time together at her elegant flagship store on a bustling corner in Buenos Aires, she shared, "I knew I wouldn't have help from the outside. My father was German, my mother was Polish, and both were immigrants. My father was a baker. They sacrificed a lot for me. My parents knew education was very important and wanted me to have the best educational opportunities.

"My mother became very sick when I was ten years old, and my parents sent me to live with my grandmother, my *oma*, who was a German immigrant. Oma had a secondary education, which was huge for a woman at the time. She was a modern woman. She read and played bridge. Though she was not caring, she was an intellectual and very different from the women of her time. Her father, my great-grandfather, had a fabric store. She told me that in her father's store they had a practice of regularly moving fabric from one side of the store to the other side. When I asked Oma why they did that, she said, "Because movement produces movement."

Marta's advice to other businesswomen is: *"Move because movement produces movement. Fear can paralyze you and then there is no movement."*

"Do you know the definition of the word *stupid* in Latin?" Marta asked looking at me with a broad smile and a glint of mischief. When I shook my head no, she continued, 'To be paralyzed.' The energy from movement gives you direction. My motivation was to be prepared to move. I studied at university and worked at the same time. I was a good student. I decided what kind of career I wanted and did the things I was able to do. When I started, success came step by step through doing things in order to survive. I am a great survivor—in all the roles, physically, emotionally, and also at work. For me, the immediate was not important. I was preparing for the long term."

ROLE MODELS

In adulthood, confidence comes from our own beliefs, from the words we use to describe our abilities and intelligence, and from the actions we personally take and from observing others succeeding. People all over the world, even the most powerful and successful among us, sometimes question themselves and their ability to succeed, just like we do. It is a rare person who does not. But how prevalent is self-doubt among women?

The Global Entrepreneurship Monitor 2012 Women's Report looked at sixty-seven countries, both developed and developing. The report found that in all sixty-seven countries women were less confident in their entrepreneurial capabilities than men, and that both men and women believe that women are not as capable in business as men![2] But in fact, when women take business risks, they succeed and fail at rates similar to those of men.[3]

Can you guess where the most confident women in the world come from?

If you thought of any developed or western country when I asked this, you are incorrect. According to the report, the women most confident about their ability to run a business live in Sub-Saharan Africa, where 67 percent trusted their ability to do so.[4] Women in this region also reported having the lowest fear of failure.[5]

What's different about Sub-Saharan Africa from other parts of the world is that it has a very high percentage of women already running businesses. This means that girls see their mothers, grandmothers, aunts, sisters, and neighbors running businesses and view it as normal. It means they have someone to teach them how to work. When the younger women see other women working and succeeding, those women become role models for them, and they start to believe that they can succeed, too. Interestingly, the highest levels of fear of failure measured by the report were experienced by women in the richer, more developed countries—not those in growth economies.[6] Just by virtue of where you live, you may be at a better starting place to be an entrepreneur.

Building confidence is about taking action. You can start building your confidence today simply by taking the next step. When women work and succeed, they build confidence. They prove to themselves that they can accomplish anything they set their minds to.

The opposite of confidence, self-doubt, only limits us as long as we let it. Yeshasvini Ramaswamy, an Indian entrepreneur who founded the leadership audit firm e2e People Practices shared how she believes the doubtful voices in our heads should be handled. "As women, we can be very judgmental—even of ourselves. We are self-critical and tend to carry a lot of baggage. Forget the voice of limitation in your head that says, *This is all I can do.* Tell your mind, 'You shut up!'"

BARRIERS TO CONFIDENCE

We undermine our confidence when we:

- Blame others when things don't go our way, instead of determining our responsibility and assessing what we could do differently or better next time.
- Expect that everything will be easy or problem free.
- Underestimate how much time, money, and hard work it will take to achieve the goals we set, such as getting a job or a promotion, or starting or growing a business.
- Ignore or fail to remember our past successes (make a point of reading your own resume or reviewing what people have said about you, once in a while).
- Try to tackle huge projects or goals all at once instead of breaking them down into manageable pieces or tasks.
- Are immobilized by our fears.
- Fail to take action in spite of our self-doubt.

A BALANCED SENSE OF CONFIDENCE

Undeterred women have an underlying and *balanced* sense of self-confidence. In my experience, this is particularly important for women in growth economies where cultural norms often dictate how women should or should not behave. Undeterred women are not arrogant or boastful. They are also not overly modest or self-denigrating, and they are willing to take credit for their contributions. Their confidence is grounded in reality and based on their skills. They know their level of expertise, which they work to improve through preparation.

Some people appear to be naturally confident, while others—even highly successful people—can lack self-confidence. A woman can be confident in some aspects of her life and not in others. For instance, she can be confident in her relationships and personal life but not as confident at work, or vice versa. Rarely, if ever, is anyone confident in every aspect of her life at all times. Undeterred women use preparation to build confidence and to move through their fear of failure.

Although Funmilayo (Funmi) Victor-Okigbo, CEO of No Surprises Events, an event production and management company in Nigeria, did not have enough prior experience, she convinced a multinational company to engage her company's services for a major event. Funmi shared that it was one of the best events they had done, an outcome she attributed to thorough preparation. "Fear of failure propelled me to deliver beyond the client's expectations." Her confidence improved once she saw what she was able to accomplish at this event through hard work.

The fierce, but quietly confident Mary Anne de Amorim Ribeiro of Sao Paulo, Brazil, is the forty-year-old founder and CEO of the early education company Pupa, as well as the mother of four kids. Earlier in her career, she ran the second largest shipping company in Brazil. "I always knew I could do anything," Mary Anne assuredly said. Since the age of five, she knew she wanted to be a working woman. "I saw the difference between the poor and the rich and I didn't like it." Her father was a priest and her mother was a seamstress. Both parents nurtured her talents, which contributed to her positive self-image. Mary Anne relayed, "I was reading at home early on and was good at math."

Mary Anne also started working at sixteen, developing further confidence in her abilities, and outweighing negative messages coming from the society around her. "I didn't let being a woman put me in a box," she resolutely said. Mary Anne quickly acquired what she describes as the "punch of playing for victory," and developed a vision for her future work with mothers and their young children.

Are you like Mary Anne and Funmi, more naturally self-confident, or do you experience a lot of self-doubt?

Whichever way you answered, why do you think this is the case?

WAYS TO BUILD YOUR CONFIDENCE

Some people believe that self-confidence is innate, an original part of someone's personality or makeup. That is not usually the case. Self-confidence can be developed. The best ways to become more confident are to think with confidence, speak with confidence, and act with confidence.

Don't wait to feel confident before beginning to act confident. Don't undermine your level of confidence with your thoughts or the way you communicate. When you act with confidence, you will begin to feel confident.

PREPARE TO BE CONFIDENT

There is a saying: "Success breeds success." I also believe that confidence breeds success. You don't have to achieve "success" to have confidence in yourself. It is, in fact, the other way around. You can choose to take steps to overcome fear even before you are successful. You will begin to experience success when you decide to have confidence in your ability to do so.

I can't blame my early childhood for any doubts I have ever faced. My parents were encouraging. Although I was overweight, wore glasses, and often had my head in a book, I made friends and did well in school. Things came easily to me in my corporate career and again when I launched and grew my coaching business. But as I started writing this book, because I was doing something new, I had a lot of self-doubt and several crises of confidence. The voice inside my head questioned my ability to write: *Who do you think you are, Rania? You are not a writer! Why do you think you can do this? What do you know about writing a book?* The truth was that I hardly knew anything about writing books, so my early attempts were not very successful. I had a lot of starts and stops. I even had to completely start over a few times.

Eventually, after much frustration and self-reproach, I realized that the primary source of my self-doubt was my lack of preparation. I had not done enough research to learn how the writing process goes for most authors. I didn't know the actual steps that a writer takes to write a book, and I had grossly underestimated how long it takes. I had assumed that because I had expertise and knew how to write business documents, I already had everything I needed to write a book. Oh, was I wrong! I had even underestimated how hard it was going to be to connect with businesswomen in places in the world where I didn't already have contacts.

After much trial and error and getting stuck for long periods of time, I realized I could change my lack of preparation. I located and began to work with a writing and business coach, Ishita Gupta. She explained the process to me, directed me to books and resources on writing, and spoke with me about my confidence. She had me start writing in small chunks, which led me to experience small successes. Each one of these actions boosted my confidence in my ability to actually get this book written.

As I implemented the strategies I had learned, I gained momentum. I started where I was and kept going. Soon I could see that I *might* be able to do it. Then I began to *believe* I could do it. I stopped blaming others for my roadblocks. As my goals became clearer, I honed my message and connected with more people who understood my vision and shared my goal of enabling women in growth economies to achieve their own definitions of professional success.

As I reflect back on all my educational experiences and my professional experiences as part of a corporation and as an entrepreneur, I now recognize that I have always prepared myself for success. Through experiences, books, talking to people, and getting training, I've learned what I needed to know. That preparation had been essential to my level of confidence and success.

NOW IT'S YOUR TURN

To prepare for success, build your confidence and address your fears. Without confidence and courage it's easy to become paralyzed and get stuck in a place that you don't believe you can get out of. Undeterred women who have developed confidence and courage keep moving forward even in the face of self-doubt. Once you have a balanced and realistic sense of self-confidence, take the other preparatory actions that will build the foundation for your success. Here's how.

SELF-REFLECTION: ARE YOU UNDERMINING YOUR CONFIDENCE?

Start by examining your thoughts and behavior. Ask:

- Do I trust myself, or am I constantly second-guessing every move I want to make?

- Do I consciously or subconsciously underestimate my abilities?

- Do I blame myself for mistakes?

- Do I negatively judge myself and regularly engage in negative self-talk?

- What does the voice inside my head say?
  - Is it critical or supportive?
  - How strong is it?
  - How much do I listen to it?

- Who or what helps me turn down or silence its negative messages?

- Do I think that people are or are not naturally confident? And have I decided that I don't have enough self-confidence to do what I want to do?

- Do I blame others, my society, culture, parents, and/or men, for my lack of achievement?

If you answered yes to any of these questions, it is an indication that you are undermining your confidence to some degree.

 ## ACTIONS
THAT BUILD CONFIDENCE

To build your self-assurance, start thinking, speaking, and acting with confidence. Pick and commit to consistently taking the actions that most resonate and apply to you from the following list of ideas, tips, and techniques.

Think with confidence. Identify your strengths, then remember them as you talk with others.

- Ask: What are my strengths?
  Examples: working with people, quantitative analysis, coming up with ideas, implementing ideas, managing projects, writing, technology, science, sales.

- Ask: What are my best characteristics or qualities? *Examples: I am very smart, kind, hardworking, exciting, thoughtful, positive, charismatic, creative, and so on.*

- Control your thoughts about yourself. With practice, you can learn to direct the way you think about yourself.
    - Use positive, kind, and encouraging words when you talk to yourself.
    - Don't dwell on mistakes you have made in the past. Instead, identify what you would do differently in the future.
    - Repeat positive statements or affirmations about yourself. Start those statements with the phrases like "I can," "I am," or "I will." *Examples: "I can get a new job," "I will get a promotion." "I can secure funding for my business." "I can accomplish this goal." "I am prepared for success." "I can see the path forward." "I am grateful for who I am and what I can accomplish." "I can change X." "I can overcome this obstacle."*
    - Mentally prepare. Come up with and rehearse the specific steps you need to take to accomplish a task.
    - Envision yourself succeeding at a task or accomplishing a goal you have set.

- Know that it is inevitable that you will not succeed at everything and that some things will go wrong. Tell yourself that mistakes and failure are normal, that you will learn from the hardships you encounter and that you are capable of finding new solutions.

- Think positively—remember that undeterred women are resilient in the face of obstacles and are able to find solutions.

Speak with confidence. Even when you don't feel completely confident, it's important to talk about your strengths, qualities, and what you can do, rather than about what you cannot do. Use phrases like: *"I can," "I am able to," "I am confident that I can," "I feel strongly that," "I know that."*

- Share how you will do a task, rather than revealing your doubts.

- Stand or a sit in the way that makes you feel confident when you are speaking.

- Don't add a question at the end of a statement or apologize when sharing your perspective.

- Say your affirmations out loud to yourself.

Act with confidence. Implement a regular confidence-building routine. These routines are proven to work for people. Select and implement ones that you believe will be most helpful to you.

- Read motivational quotes.

- Read books that give you ideas, hope, and inspiration.

- Exercise.

- Dress in a way that makes you feel more confident.

- Write down your affirmations and put them in places at home and work where you can see them.

- Establish a meditation practice during which you focus on your affirmations, confidence, and goals, and on your gratitude for what you are capable of and have already achieved.

- Build your knowledge and skills. Specific ways to build your competence will be covered in Chapter 4.

- Practice what you plan to say or do. Sometimes I practice in front a of mirror so I can see myself saying the words, and can work on my tone of voice and my body language.

- Observe people you deem confident. How do they behave? Adopt or adapt similar behaviors that boost your level of confidence.

- Make an appointment with someone confident whom you admire. Ask her (or him) how she builds her self-confidence.

- Challenge yourself to do things professionally that you are not comfortable doing.

- Try. Even if you are not sure you can succeed, even if you have self-doubt or reservation. As long as you have prepared, move forward.

- Accept responsibility for failures and learn from your mistakes, but don't blame yourself or doubt your ability to succeed in the future.

- Stretch yourself by taking an additional step beyond what you normally take after achieving success with something you are good at. Ask: What else would I do if I felt confident?

Stay tuned for more on confidence, as I will cover it again in later chapters.

SUMMARY

You have the ability to develop your self-confidence. By reprogramming your brain to reduce negative thoughts and emotions, and taking the risk to move toward your goals every day, you will begin to trust this capacity. You will then be able to pursue your goals even if you still have some self-doubt. Each of your accomplishments, no matter how small it is, will build the confidence you need to tackle larger and more difficult challenges.

Confidence is built step by step through thought, word, and deed. Practice thinking with confidence by quieting your self-judging inner voice. Practice speaking with confidence by using self-affirming phrases with a strong, open posture. Act with confidence by learning new skills and trying new things. The more you think, speak, and act with confidence, the more confident you will feel.

MOVE
THROUGH
FEAR

CHAPTER 3

COURAGE

Keep going. You will find your courage
on the other side of your fears.

WHAT RIGHT DO I OR ANYONE ELSE HAVE TO teach you about courage—you, who are already so courageous? You live in a part of the world that is rapidly developing and so much is changing. You may live in a part of the world where there is political or civil unrest. It is likely that you live in a place where men have most of the power and women still face various forms of gender inequities—some visible and others hidden. If this is so, then you have shown courage in pursuing an education and a career and in advocating for yourself and in having bold aspirations.

I honor, admire, acknowledge, and respect your courage. Even so, I want to talk with you about taking your courage to a new level. I want to help you realize that you can tap into the courage you already have to tackle the new obstacles and challenges you will encounter on the journey to achieve your professional and business goals.

Courage is acting even when you are afraid. When you are courageous, you persist when others in similar circumstances would give up. Courage enables undeterred women to find the solutions to overcome obstacles. Their courage comes from their preparation, confidence, and motivation, as well as from the people with whom they spend time.

In the report "Unleashing the Power of Women Entrepreneurs," the multinational professional services firm EY concludes, "Even when there are no legal barriers to starting a business, courage is still required. As the Global Entrepreneurship Monitor (GEM) has documented, "Perceptual factors that reflect optimism, self-confidence, and reduced fear of failure are important predictors of women's entrepreneurship."[1] In this, women are no different from men. Both women and men who launch businesses tend to be optimists with a high tolerance for risk. Yet, even among entrepreneurs, there is a gender gap in confidence. Women are often more afraid of failure.[2] GEM has identified the most important factors that encourage women to put aside their fears and start a business. Interestingly enough, household income and educational attainment are not as important as two other factors:

- Being employed.
- Having a network that includes other entrepreneurs.[3]

FEAR

Most often our hesitation to boldly pursue what we want comes from fear. I have observed in myself and picked up from my conversations with women around the world that most of us are not held back by a lack of ability or confidence, but by our fears. What are we afraid of? We fear that we might fail. That perhaps we are not smart enough, good enough, connected enough, liked enough, or *whatever* enough (insert your own thought) to succeed.

According to the GEM 2012 Women's Report, in every region of the world, women are more afraid of failure, on average, than their male counterparts.[4] Some of the most developed regions have the highest levels of fear of failure, including developed regions of Asia, Israel, and Europe.[5] The fear of failure is linked to lower rates of entrepreneurship among women.[6]

Most people are really good at disguising and denying their fears. We often label fear as a lack of something such as time, opportunity, knowledge, or support. (Each of us uses her own labels.) Often we'll focus upon or talk about the obstacles in our paths rather than the core issue preventing us from overcoming those obstacles, which is our fear.

Face it, the more opportunities you want and the bigger your dreams, the more uncomfortable you are likely going to feel.

Although Celeste North, a tech entrepreneur in Latin America, once ran out of money and lost a business partner at the same time, she counts fear as her biggest obstacle to date.

She said, "In the end, even though it may be hard to find, there is always a solution for all kinds of problems. But if you let the uncertainty and fear beat you, you are done. Bouncing back from fear is harder than overcoming difficult circumstances."

Naturally, women like May Khoury in Jordan, whose husband died when her children were still young, and Alena Vladimirskaya in Russia, whose husband left her when she was eight months pregnant, were afraid for their futures. But neither let her fears paralyze her.

DIFFERENT TYPES OF FEAR

Fear is a natural reaction. The fear response is a critical instinct for self-preservation. Rational fears enable us to respond to threats. Irrational fears, by contrast, stop us from taking the bold actions or calculated risks that could result in a positive outcome. Professionally, our fears tend to be strongest when we perceive that an outcome will have a deep impact on us, when we care strongly about what happens. Sometimes professional fear is justified, but often it is irrational and unjustified. Three of the biggest fears I see in women are the fear of rejection, fear of mistakes, and fear of failure. There is also a fourth big fear, which often goes unrecognized: the fear of success.

Fear of rejection. If you fear rejection, it is virtually impossible to be an entrepreneur. Like all entrepreneurs, Wee Yen Lim took a big risk. Remember her? She left her corporate consulting job in Malaysia and moved to Mexico. Then, although she did not speak Spanish, she decided to start a business. Talk about courage! As you can imagine, she initially faced a lot of rejection. But the undeterred Wee Yen believes, "Rejection won't kill you. If someone doesn't respond to you, then all it means is that the time has not yet come for you to work with them."

Fear of mistakes. I work with women all the time who don't act, or fail to take risks in their careers or businesses because they erroneously seek perfection or are afraid of the ramifications of making a mistake. Fortunately, I was cured of the fear of making mistakes early in my career.

I began my career at the financial institution that became Bank of America. I have nothing but good memories of being supported by people at the bank, being given developmental opportunities and recognition of my work. The supportive culture enabled me to accomplish many things that I am proud of to this day. I attribute my achievements to the bank's culture that valued honest, well-thought-out efforts, even if employees sometimes made mistakes.

The first time I heard this value expressed, I couldn't believe it. I had made a mistake at work. After I fearfully shared what had happened with my manager, he said, *"Great, you are making all the right mistakes!"*

Completely taken off guard, I asked, "What? What does that even mean?"

My boss then explained that although I had researched the issue and thought through what I knew, when I connected the dots and took action, there were a couple of things I still did not know and had no way of knowing. That's why the actions I took didn't work out. My boss was celebrating my mistake because he knew I was challenging myself to move outside my comfort zone. He said he knew I'd gain valuable insight from that mistake, and that I couldn't have learned the new information if I had not pushed myself to try.

During my career at the bank, I made many more mistakes and had several other bosses say the same thing to me. I'm forever grateful to them and the bank for instilling this value in me. Seventeen years later, I am still making mistakes. I always hope they are the "right" ones.

Understanding that it is okay to make mistakes gives me the courage to take action in spite of my fears. The experiences I had at the bank gave me the courage to take bold actions throughout my career and remind me to be courageous in the future.

Argentinian entrepreneur Marta Harff talks about working through the fear of making mistakes in this way: "Mistakes— everybody will make some. The greatest enemy is fear of mistakes. You can survive if you can learn from your mistakes. Too bad many people don't allow themselves to make mistakes."

South African corporate leader Tantaswa Fubu has a similar view of mistakes. She says, "I am not afraid to make mistakes. I learn from them, I also share the lessons I learn with others so that both the firm and those individuals can benefit from my experiences. I do not believe that my mistakes define me. I am also not afraid to say, 'I do not know, teach me.'"

Fear of failure. Unmana Datta, the Indian woman you met in Chapter 1, didn't let fear stop her. Both she and her husband quit their jobs to start Markitty, an online marketing tool for small businesses that put together analytics from Facebook, Twitter, and Google, and suggested actions to take. Unfortunately, the company failed. On her blog, Unmana shared, "We wanted to build a product that would help small businesses do better marketing, to build a great small business, and to help people get more out of their marketing. We failed. We haven't seen a way forward for a while. The decision to quit was a difficult one, but we decided to choose our time rather than wait until we had no way out and would have to stop anyway.

"Since then, my husband and I moved to Mumbai and started new jobs. We are still doing things we are interested in (project management and marketing, respectively). Our year of entrepreneurship taught us so much. We are glad we took the plunge and put everything we had into something we believed in so that we tested our limits. During that year, we met wonderful people and learned more about ourselves."

Today, Unmana works on the marketing team at one of the largest IT companies in the world, Tata Consultancy Services.

In China, Yvonne Chow who works for Polymer Group, Inc., a multinational corporation that engineers nonwoven fabrics used for various hygienic, medical, and industrial purposes, shared that a few months after she became a senior sales director she had to give up the sales part of her job. She reflected, "Accepting the fact that I am not capable enough is not that tough, but making the decision to give it up is tough. I understand that facing failure is also part of life. The longer I struggle, the less chance we have for our commercial team to win."

Fear of success. According to Marianne Williamson, "Our deepest fear is not that we are inadequate. Our deepest fear is that we are powerful beyond measure. It is our light, not our darkness that most frightens us."[6] Sometimes our fears have to do with what will happen and what others will say about us, if and when we succeed. We can feel pressure not to lose what we have, the pressure of people watching us closely, or the pressure of serving as a role model to other women or to our children. We worry about making a wrong turn and losing what we've already gained.

To counter this fear, Indian entrepreneur Yeshasvini Ramaswamy, says, "We have to forget all our limitations and the idea that 'This is all I can do.' We are so scared. We have everything—the talent, the will—but sometimes we become lazy and use fear as an excuse.

MOVE PAST FEAR

There is a misperception that successful people don't experience fear. This is simply not the case. Everyone, even the most successful person, has fears. A difference between more successful people and less successful people is that those who succeed don't allow fear to stop them from taking calculated risks to accomplish their objectives. You don't overcome fear. Rather, you work through your fears by identifying what you are afraid of, doing what you can to mitigate the negative outcome you fear, and then moving forward.

Take the story that I heard tall, elegant, and poised Aisha Alfardan relay at the inaugural Qatar International Business Women's Forum, a conference attended by 450 professional women from across the Middle East. Aisha began her career at the Commercial Bank of Qatar. She then later joined Alfardan Automobiles to assist her father and brothers with their family business. Aisha drove a car before women in Qatar could get licensed to drive (like some women in Saudi Arabia do today). When the laws changed, her experience of driving, as well as her knowledge of women's tastes, prompted her to ask if Alfardan Automobiles would order some very specific colors and styles of cars that would appeal to the newly licensed female drivers. The all-male management of the car dealership disagreed with her recommendations and did not want to order the cars. Although she was afraid of failing, she had the courage to stand alone in her convictions. Since she was unable to convince them in any other way, Aisha took a big risk and committed to buying any unsold cars herself. She was fortunate to have the financial wherewithal to do so. The cars were ordered and her male colleagues took bets as to how many cars would not sell.

You can guess how this story ends—of course, all the cars sold! Aisha increased sales at Alfardan Automobiles and then became Director of Business Development.

Many people think that waiting to act helps you feel less afraid. That is usually not the case. You are better off moving forward in spite of your fear, even if that means taking tiny steps. You have to decide that what you want is more important than the fears you feel.

That's what Regina Agyare did when she left a good IT job at a bank in Ghana to start her own business. All she heard were negative comments like "You will probably come back. You should wait until you are older, until you have more assets . . ." She was nervous, but she made her move anyway. Ironically, her first client was the bank where she used to work.

WAYS TO CULTIVATE COURAGE

Where does courage come from? The three best ways to cultivate your courage are to be clear about your motivation for action, to surround yourself with other people who, like you, are seeking to be courageous and to have routines that help them move past their fears. To demonstrate courage, you have to be prepared to act. We build our courage when we are self-motivated, confident in our capabilities, and surround ourselves with other courageous people.

COURAGE COMES FROM MOTIVATION

Another difference between people who seem always to achieve their goals and those who never do is the intensity of their inner drive. Think about some of the successful people you know.

If they are like the ones I know, they work long hours, day after day. They read voraciously and talk constantly about the topics that interest them. They do not need to have anyone standing behind them pushing them forward because they are pushing themselves. Mostly the difference between the people who succeed and the people that don't is execution. Successful women have an ability to persevere and get done whatever needs to be done. They believe in themselves and their goals, and have a strong desire to succeed.

Self-motivation is what keeps you on track to achieve the objectives that are personally fulfilling to you, even if no one is looking. It is an internal force pushing you to go on, to achieve, and to keep moving forward no matter what. The key to being motivated like this—to take action on your own without encouragement or prompting from others—is to know *why* you want what you want, not just *what* you want.

Crystal Yi Wang, Associate Director at Deloitte Financial Advisory Service, was born in China in early 1981. She described the origins of her motivation by explaining, "We are the first generation born and raised after China's economy reform and the first generation with the one-baby policy. Both my parents' early lives were impacted by the political and economic changes in China. They had no chance for a good education, no opportunity for a career, and no dreams for themselves. I observed my parents' lives, and one day I realized that I would never want to become like them. Never! Most of my female cousins were their families' only children, so they were never treated differently than sons. They were raised with the same standards a man would be. My parents never treated me differently as a woman, never told me, "Since you are a woman, all you need is an easy life." My first motivation for success came when I was twenty years old and had the realization that I wanted to have my own dreams, to live for myself, not for others, and I wanted my own success."

Undeterred women know why they do what they do, and they have the drive to show for it. Their drive comes from having positive thoughts and aspirations for a better future for themselves, their families, and their communities, and for some women, for the world at large.

Indian entrepreneur Yeshasvini Ramaswamy explained this last particular motivation in the following way. "It's better when a woman can be a role model for her son. It changes a person's life forever. We have a long way to go for women's empowerment in India, but it will create a whole generation of citizens who are more inclusive in their thought. So it is very important for me that we are changing more and more lives in that way."

Reem Asaad, a financial advisor in Saudi Arabia, summed up her motivation by saying, "I always keep in my mind that how I live my life today will leave a long-lasting mark on my daughters' lives and the lives of women and men in generations to come."

For others, like architect Shahira Fahmy, motivation comes from a desire to leave a legacy. In Shahira's case, the legacy is an "eye piece. More than a building, it's something that makes a difference, a building that is the part of Cairo's future heritage."

Ghanaian tech entrepreneur Regina Agyare wants to leave a different type of legacy. With immense hope in her voice, she shared, "Even though I had access to good schools and so on, there are still a lot of people in Ghana who don't have things that they need. There needs to be a change, and we can change. One of the things that motivate me is that we have so much potential here and it isn't being used. When I wake up every morning, I have to do more. It's a calling that I have: I have to leave a legacy behind."

For other women, like Argentine entrepreneur Marta Harff, motivation is her unapologetic desire to make money and survive.

External forces can be motivating, too: deadlines, the need to pay your bills, the promises you made to a customer or client, or to your boss. There are many real reasons that impel you to act. When you are very clear about your reasons for an action that you want to take, no one has to ask you to do anything. No one has to ask you to work hard. You want to, and you can't help yourself; you just do it and keep doing it—you are self-motivated.

You, and women like you, are my motivation. When I work long hours and on weekends, I am thinking about you, what I want to convey to you, and how best to share what I have to say. This doesn't feel like work to me. As I write this sentence, I'm aware that I've already tried four times to stop writing for the day. I've even shut my laptop computer and walked away. But each time I did, I came back and opened it up again because I thought of something else I wanted to tell you.

I can't begin to capture all the reasons women choose to work. Reasons include necessity, financial rewards, opportunities to contribute, and the desire to be recognized and make a difference. An additional motivation weighs heavily on many of the women I spoke with: the desire to be a positive role model for other women and for their children. The key is to be aware of your motivations and to own them. Remind yourself of them often. They can drive you to work differently and better.

COURAGE COMES FROM SUPPORT

Undeterred women have support networks that encourage them to be courageous and stay motivated as they pursue their goals. They make a point of spending time with people who believe in them and encourage their professional success.

Some women are lucky enough to have strong support from their families. The seeds of South African Wendy Luhabe's courage came from her mother. Wendy's mom left her husband in the mid-1960s, at a time when separation and divorce were largely unheard of. Wendy saw that her mother's action required a big dose of courage to put up with being judged by the community. Through her mother's action, Wendy learned that you don't have to stay in a relationship if it does not work.

When Wendy was a girl, her mother moved to a new town far away from her friends and relatives and started working as a qualified midwife and nurse. Not only did Wendy observe her mother's courage, she saw that her mother had marketable skills she could rely on. Wendy's mother was among the first generation of women in South Africa to take out an insurance policy. She introduced Wendy and her siblings to financial management at an early age.

During our interview, Wendy calmly shared, "In my formative years, I was exposed to my mother's resilience. I witnessed her fulfilling her aspirations at a time when women were expected to 'know their place.' My mother refused and challenged the stereotype of women so it became natural for me to grow up as an independent woman and assume I could achieve anything I wanted. That was all I ever knew." You may recall that Wendy went on to cofound the first female-owned company to be listed on the Johannesburg Stock Exchange.

In the Dominican Republic, Estefany Marte joined her father in his fruit and vegetable business, and helped him grow it. When Estefany talked fondly about how her father encouraged her to do things in her own way, she shared that although she made mistakes, her father supported the decisions she made. "One of the times my father did this was a couple of years ago, after I hired a group of women to peel some fruit," Estefany said. "I did not investigate the average rate for this type of work and ended up paying the women more than triple the going rate. This was a loss for the company and it led to more problems when we wanted to adjust the rate for the women, because of course, they wanted to keep making what I had originally paid them. I apologized to my father and told him I would pay for the difference in rate. He said that this was a big part of learning, that he appreciated my honesty and felt sure I would never do that again. I never did."

She continued, "On another occasion, I made some communication mistakes while negotiating with a supplier. I did not write down the conditions we discussed and the supplier denied us some of the benefits he had offered. My father told me to always write things down, at least on my cell phone. Since then, I even use Post-Its®, pieces of paper, and my iPhone . . . anything to make sure I keep track of the conditions agreed upon with my suppliers."

Successful businesswomen in emerging economies (and in many other countries around the world) also often talk about their supportive husbands. Half-jokingly, but with a real underlying truth, many women claim that a supportive husband is the most important factor in a woman's professional success. When I probe further, asking women what type of supportive behavior they most value from their husbands, often the first thing on their list is not the amount of time their husbands spend with their children or doing chores around the house; rather it's the emotional support their mates provide. Receiving emotional support from their husbands and other people around them gives women the courage to pursue bold professional goals and dreams.

Although many women have supportive families, not all women do. For many women in growth economies, there are prevailing messages from people around them to get married, be a good wife, have children, and devote themselves to caring for their extended family. Perhaps you have heard this type of advice, too. Some parents and extended family members repeatedly urge their daughters to "find something easier." One woman entrepreneur from the Middle East whom I met at a conference captured it by saying, "My mother always complains that I work too hard. 'Why do you do this to yourself? Why don't you get married?' she asks."

In addition to families who don't fully support the career interests of their daughters, wives, or sisters, I have also seen the diminishing effect that a woman's friends can have on her professional goals and courage. When a woman is surrounded primarily by female relations and friends who are not working, or who don't agree with her professional aspirations, they can put pressure on her not to work or not to work "too hard." If so, she may become discouraged and start to doubt her ability to succeed. She may come to feel that it will be too hard to manage her career along with all the other expectations that society places on her as a woman. I've seen and heard women question themselves and wonder, *Who am I to think I can do this when friends/family are not?*

When our goals are different from or greater than the goals of most people around us, we can feel like we have no right to want what we want. We can start to feel guilty for having ambitions.

Wendy Luhabe shared this sage advice, derived from her experiences: "Don't expect to have much support early in your new venture. In the beginning, you will be on your own. You will need to rely on your own passion, sense of adventure, and commitment to support and sustain you until you achieve success or have a breakthrough. Difficulties and deceptions are often fostered by those wishing to discourage individuals who don't have experience. Don't let them disrupt you."

Ultimately, you need to dig deep within yourself to succeed when the odds seem against you. When your environment, society, culture, or people make it difficult for you to succeed, you have to find your motivations and decide to keep going and take the next step. You'll need to motivate yourself to find the solution or the pathway toward achieving what you want. This may also require working around the obstacles in your way. Finding ways to motivate yourself is your personal responsibility.

None of us can or should expect support from family and friends, nor can we entirely rely on it. However, in addition to our own self-motivation, we feel emboldened to take more courageous actions when we surround ourselves and spend time with people who understand, support, and encourage us.

COURAGE COMES FROM RITUALS AND ROUTINES

You've probably heard and seen athletes, actors, or musicians go through a set of rituals and routines before they perform or compete in an event. Like them, those of us in the business world need to have our own processes for handling our nerves and moving past the things we are afraid of. One of my practices is to do a lot of research before I tackle things that are new, challenging, or important to me. I read everything I can get my hands on. The information serves as a sort of armor of strength that helps me face my fear.

Other people address their fears by talking with people they trust, praying or meditating, or by implementing a specific routine that they have come up with. Routines that people develop for the purpose of calming their fears typically have particular specifics steps, including eating and drinking certain foods and beverages—or fasting—reading a certain passage from a book, reciting a poem they have memorized, listening to something particular, saying affirmations, and/or wearing particular clothing. Actions like these can help you become more courageous.

NOW IT'S YOUR TURN

In this chapter, we've covered three very important strategies to prepare for success: moving forward in spite of your fears, identifying your motivations, and having a strong support system. The following exercises are designed to help you take your courage to a new level.

(?)   ## SELF-REFLECTION: HOW CAN YOU BRING YOUR FEARS INTO THE OPEN?

If you can accurately identify your fears and pinpoint why they exist, you can address them and make more rational business decisions. It doesn't matter whether you fear rejection, failure, or something else. Bringing your fear out into the open is the first step. Knowing is better than not knowing.

Here are some questions to ask.

- What do I fear the most?
  Examples: failure, financial instability, or not being able to find another job.

- What am I worried about?
  Examples: what people will say about me, my reputation, that failure is not understood or acceptable in my country.

- What is the worst that could happen if I proceed with my goal?
  Examples: I could lose my job or run out of money.

- Why am I afraid I can't succeed?
  Example: I don't think I have all the information, skills, or contacts I need.

- What am I afraid will happen if I become really successful?
  Example: People will think I care more about my career than my family.

- Why am I afraid that I won't be able to manage at home if I am successful?
  Examples: I don't have a supportive husband or family.

ACTIONS
TO BUILD COURAGE

After you have answered the self-reflection questions, then:

- Identify what makes you feel strong.
  Examples: having knowledge and information, building time into my schedule to research and gather information.

- Build rituals, practices, or processes that help you work through your fears.
  Examples: doing research, talking with people I trust, praying, or meditating.

---

⑦ SELF-REFLECTION: WHAT MOTIVATES YOU?

You will build your ability to take courageous action only when you know why you want what you want. Think about what motivates you. Ask: "What motivates me?" Is it any of the following things?

- A sense of achievement
- Recognition
- Money
- Power
- Influence
- Having independence
- Learning and mastering new things
- Setting an example
- Having a sense of purpose or making a difference
- Wanting to leave a legacy

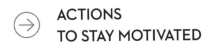

ACTIONS
TO STAY MOTIVATED

Any time you encounter an obstacle or a personal detractor, any time you are afraid, think about the reasons behind your work. When you focus on why something is so important to you, you will be more able to find solutions to get what you want. You will also have the courage to take action in spite of the difficulties or your fears.

SELF-REFLECTION:
DO YOU NEED MORE SUPPORT?

Supportive people around you will encourage you, and enable you, to take courageous action. To create a support system, ask:

- Are the people around me supportive of my professional aspirations?

- Am I spending time with people who have similar goals as I have, both in type and in size?

If the answer to either of these questions is no, take some or all of the following actions.

ACTIONS
TO BUILD YOUR SUPPORT

Here are some ways to build the support you need.

- Seek out friends and extended family members, both male and female, who are working, perhaps including professors from your university. Speak with them about your professional aspirations.

- Join business organizations that provide services for women and social networks that support women's careers and/or businesses online and in person.

- Reach out to connect with working women in your country and region. These could be peers or women who have already established themselves professionally.

- Connect and build a relationship with someone who can be a mentor to you.

- Read about the professional paths of other working women. You can find lots of examples online, including at TheWayWomenWork.com.

- Ignore or get away from people who put you down or don't believe in your abilities.

- Professionally surround yourself, with people who have positive outlooks and similar goals to yours.

- Spend time with professionals (mentors and others) who are doing things that are similar to what you want to do. These should be people who believe in you and encourage your success.

Later in this book I will provide additional information about building your support network and describe specific ways to cultivate supportive relationships.

SUMMARY

The remedy for fear is action. You will succeed if you face what you are afraid of and continue to move toward your goals no matter what type of challenges you encounter. To take action when you feel afraid, simply push yourself to go one step beyond the point where your instincts tell you to stop. Then take one more step beyond that. And then . . . you guessed it . . . one more after that. As you do so, you'll see that you are capable of moving forward in spite of fear.

Fear and doubt cannot be entirely eradicated; they will always continue to exist alongside our actions as we move toward our goals. The good news is that when we pursue our purpose, we stop fueling our fears and doubts. Fear is not actually something to overcome; it is an emotion to work through.

Remember, no one can motivate you as much as you can motivate yourself. If you want to succeed, be resilient and undeterred. You can also gain courage from other people. It is therefore important to surround yourself with people who appreciate and respect your aspirations, and to keep your distance from those who don't.

NOTES

KEEP
LEARNING

CHAPTER 4

COMPETENCE

"Be so good at what you do, that gender won't matter."
Funmilayo Victor-Okigbo
Nigerian event planner

NOTHING CLOSES THE OPPORTUNITY AND INCOME gaps between men and women, and between rich and poor people, more effectively than education.[1] But access to education and development opportunities is far from equal for men and women in developing nations, with women in rural areas granted the least access. If you are like the majority of women reading this book, you are one of the fortunate women who have an education.

As a young woman, Saudi Arabian Dr. Manar Al-Moneef became very concerned about the health of people in her country. Driven by the desire to make a difference in the healthcare needs of her country, she pursued a medical education, which culminated in her also earning a doctorate in molecular oncology and genetics. Many people derided her for her decision to pursue this course of study and her professional path. She was repeatedly told, "No one will want to marry you if you do this." The courage to pursue what was important to her came from her motivation. "God puts us on Earth for a purpose. This is mine," she said.

Her ability to achieve what was important to her came from the knowledge and skills she built through learning— her *competence*. Dr. Al-Moneef put countless hours into her education and into doing well in her early career assignments. She read everything she could put her hands on that might help her people, and participated in the most difficult medical challenges she could find. Her competence was recognized and rewarded. If Dr. Al-Moneef had not been a lifelong learner, she would never have gone as far as she has in her career or made the difference she has in the healthcare arena in Saudi Arabia.

Undeterred women are perpetual students. Because they operate in a continual learning mode, they are highly competent in their fields. Like them, you already have a strong foundation to be a lifelong learner. You built those skills in school and university. What is required now and throughout your career is to continue practicing the same habits you developed as a student. Just as you did at school, you need to keep learning to succeed at work.

When I asked about her successful career path, Vania Neves, a senior information technology (IT) manager at a multinational company in Brazil, responded calmly, confidently, and very pragmatically, *"It was my plan."* Vania is a black Brazilian and comes from a family of modest means. We spoke about the experience of being black in a country deeply scarred by a history of racial discrimination and where today inequality continues to exist. In true undeterred fashion, she expressed pride in being black, but spoke about how she does not allow her race to dominate or shape her thinking. What does guide her is her mother's oft-repeated adage, *"If you want something, be ready."*

To Vania and her mother, *being ready* means always being prepared for what you want. In Vania's case that originally meant studying very hard in high school so she could earn the high grades that would allow her to attend a public university. Unlike in some countries, public universities in Brazil are the top institutions and the most desirable schools to attend. Vania's grades got her into a public university, where she excelled in her coursework.

In her career, Vania employs a similar approach. Every time she wants a new job or opportunity, she takes it upon herself to learn as much as she can about it and to develop the necessary skills. Since she wanted to achieve a senior management role, she knew she had to build her competencies. She had to learn English so she could read, write, and speak it well. Today, she excels in English. When she wanted to do more public speaking, she took presentation classes. In 2012, she spoke at a NASA conference. She has invested and continues to invest her own time and, when necessary, her own money to learn skills that enable her to contribute in new ways. Even now, in spite of the fact that she is one of the most senior corporate women in Brazil, she is working toward a master's degree and attends classes at night.

BUILD YOUR COMPETENCIES

The third component of being prepared is competence. You build competence when you expand your base of knowledge and continually acquire and improve the skills you need to succeed. In fact, for many people, competence is what enables them to be confident and have courage.

Advances in technology have led to fast rates of change in every country and every industry. This means that while what we learned yesterday is still very important, we will always need to acquire new knowledge. We cannot be lulled into thinking that we already know enough to be successful. We have to learn new things today, tomorrow, the next day, and every day. To succeed, we have to be not just current, but ahead. Lynn De Souza, former Chairman and CEO of Lintas Media Group, one of India's largest media agencies, explained it like this: "There are so many challenges ahead, so much to learn, and so much to do. The only people who can be on top of all this are those who want to keep learning and keep evolving and keep traveling. There is no place for those who think they have arrived. My best work is yet to come."

Regardless of what type of career or business you are pursuing or intend to pursue, learn about the key areas of business, for instance, how a business makes money, sales, operations, and technology. It is especially important to know and understand how a business makes money and what drives its performance. Rwandan entrepreneur Jessie Kalisa Umutoni, the managing director of G-MART Limited, a school chalk manufacturing company, describes her learning process and why it mattered. "I would spend my days in factories learning how things are manufactured, how factories are run, and studying the market. For any business to succeed, a person first has to learn about the business and the market they are targeting."[2]

Also determine what knowledge and skills will be needed in your field in the future. Focus your lifelong learning in these areas. When Ana Kolarević, the founder of Sizem, the app that "loves your boobs," first decided to become an entrepreneur, she researched business startup procedures in Zagreb, Croatia, studied marketing, and polished her public speaking skills. "I looked for programmers, and researched whatever I could about IT and doing business. I also read about other entrepreneurs and their experiences. Then I started developing a business plan and a budget, and doing more research on my customer's needs and the benefits and manufacturing processes of comparable products, such as why bras work and how they are made," Ana said. "Once I got used to it, I learned that I really enjoyed pitching to potential investors. Now, presenting to others on stage is one of my favorite things. I especially like pitching in English."

Her hard work paid off. Ana won a couple of pitch competitions and found a team of three computer programmers to establish her company's online presence. She also connected with a woman who was a bra expert to help develop the Sizem app, which helps women accurately determine their bra size and then promotes products that work for them. She also won entrance into three high-profile tech startup events in Berlin, Vienna, and London. Her multifaceted approach to learning really paid off for her.

Christine Khasinah-Odero, entrepreneur and founder of Supamamas.co.ke, an online portal for local goods that a mother and child might need, attributes an essential part of her success to having the skills and ability to see a need in the Kenyan marketplace. Christine first began to develop her expertise by majoring in marketing and then continuing on to get a master's degree in business administration from Liverpool University. She shared that her experiences in college encouraged her to be a freethinker and to come up with new ideas. Prior to becoming an entrepreneur, Christine held positions where she developed the management and leadership skills that enabled her to run Supamamas.

WAYS TO LEARN

Opportunities to learn take many forms. Recognize and take advantage of opportunities to learn at work, from others, through online resources, at conferences, in training programs, and through books. Don't wait for someone to make these opportunities available to you. Undeterred women take the responsibility and initiative for their own growth and development. Here are the four primary ways you can continually learn.

Experience. The absolute best way to learn is by doing. More than any other developmental activity, including the ones that follow, the best possible way to expand your base of knowledge is to have a variety of experiences. You will learn the most when you take on new and more challenging assignments, start something new, fix something at work that is not going well, grow or expand a client relationship or business, work in another country (even for a short time), and change your areas of responsibility in order to develop broad experiences in multiple parts of an organization.

You will learn more from having actual professional experiences than you will from activities like training programs, mentoring, conferences, and reading. Where and how do you get actual experience? You ask for it! You volunteer for hard assignments. You tell your manager you want them and if necessary, or you simply want to, you can also change jobs to get them.

Renata Pessoa, now a managing director at Accenture in Brazil, brazenly pursued several development opportunities early in her career. She told me, "At the beginning of my career, I was selected to be a trainee at a prominent wholesale bank. The selection process was very competitive. It was even more competitive than my university admission process, with something like twenty candidates per opening. Everything was going well at the bank until there was an acquisition. After the acquisition, everything changed. I had already made up my mind that I wanted to work in the mergers and acquisitions

(M&A) area instead of the department I was working in. So I asked for a meeting with my director and someone from the human resources department. I told them I'd like to move to M&A. Because of everything that was going on at the bank, I was told I would have to wait for four to six months before they could consider my request, and even then there was no promise that my request for a transfer would be honored.

"Despite the fact that the Brazilian market was suffering from a very high unemployment rate, I decided to resign from the bank and sell everything I had in order to live and study in Boston for four months. (I only had enough money to spend four months there.) I felt the experience would be essential not only to expanding my view of the world, but also for improving my English skills and helping me better define my professional goals."

Renata's experiences led her to make the decision to leave the banking field and instead pursue a career in management consulting. Renata is a self-directed learner who has also participated in several training programs including a one-year, global women's fellowship program. The competencies she developed and the contributions she made were recognized by Accenture, and after a series of promotions Renata became a managing director, one of the most senior roles in this company.

Engage with people. There are many ways to learn from other people, including working directly for or with them, observing them from a distance, shadowing them closely (as an intern or apprentice would), reading about them, and of course, asking them questions directly.

Indian entrepreneur Yeshasvini Ramaswamy learns by asking people. "I always seek help. I know I am not perfect, so I am shameless about asking for help."

Chinese marketing director Michelle Wang learns by listening to and interacting with people. "Having interacted with people across the world has really helped me change the way I think. I realize how important it is to listen and to understand other people's perspectives. The more I hear from others, the less I feel I know. The open mind and honest attitude I developed during my years abroad have benefited me greatly throughout my career journey so far."

Even if you cannot directly engage with people, you can observe what they do. Regina Agyare, the tech entrepreneur from Ghana whom you met in Chapter 3, used that approach. "I haven't had mentors. Generally, I am motivated by people I observe and my surroundings."

Get feedback. Another great way to develop your expertise is to get regular feedback. I've observed that early in people's careers they ask for and are given regular feedback. As they progress into more senior roles, they are given and ask for feedback less and less frequently.

Soliciting feedback is up to you; it is your responsibility to regularly seek it. Senior and executive managers and others sometimes do not give specific, actionable feedback because they don't know how, don't take the time, or believe they should not have to. They may want to avoid offending or discouraging the people they work with, especially when it comes to giving feedback to women.

Like their senior managers or executives who don't give enough feedback, for a host of reasons some women (and men) don't ask for feedback. They may erroneously believe that if people had feedback to give them they would do so, that people at their title or level don't need to ask for feedback, or that they can self-assess and know what they should be doing. In some cases, they don't know how or when to ask for feedback. Sometimes they are afraid of what they will hear or that they won't know how to address the feedback they get. I have found that the higher up in an organization people are, the less frequently they ask for feedback.

Sometimes, of course, the opposite is true, as in the case of one of my former clients who constantly asks for feedback. In this client's case, the request for feedback is actually a cover for wanting to be told and reassured that she is doing well.

Originally from Algeria, in North Africa, Leila Rezaiguia had seventeen years of corporate experience before she became an entrepreneur. She is passionate and outspoken by nature, and grew up in a family she describes as very direct. Her experiences in the oil and gas industry and financial services and her expertise in human resources led to jobs in Abu Dhabi and Dubai. In one of her roles as a liaison to the CEO, board of directors, and executive committee, she learned that it was crucial for her to be diplomatic in office politics. This style of communication did not come naturally to her and although it was very difficult for her, she recognized that she needed to develop these skills in order to succeed and advance in her job.

Leila started learning how to be diplomatic by watching people she knew were successful in this area. She also talked to her mentor, who is her father. As the chief financial officer for forty-two years at a company with 100,000-plus employees, Leila's father knew well the importance of diplomacy. Leila told me, "I was struggling. My dad kept telling me I had to mellow my communication approach. I learned a lot from him; especially that you have to be really, really patient—otherwise you really can't do business in this region." Leila now owns her career counseling business. The patience and diplomacy skills she developed serve her well as she builds her business in the Middle East.

Read. Successful people all around the world have an insatiable curiosity to learn what's new, and they read to stay informed. They stay current on trends in their industries and in the marketplace at large, and make reading a regular practice and part of their weekly schedule.

I love to learn by reading. Growing up, my parents never told my brother, sister, and me to go outside and play, or to do our chores. Instead we were always told, "Go read a book." As a result, I developed a love for reading and it became one of my most cherished and useful habits. I consider my lifelong reading habit an essential component of my success, a source of confidence, and an aspect of my working-through-fear routine. I start every morning by catching up on what's new and going on in business around the world, and I voraciously keep up to date on developments in my field and with all types of matters regarding businesswomen in growth economies by reading blogs and news journals.

One of my clients has a standing practice of locating ten different articles a week from sources outside her field that interest her although they have no direct correlation with her work. She does not end the week without reading all of them.

Lyubov Simonova, a Russian venture capitalist, relayed that she typically reads two or more business books per month to get ideas and inspiration. Those twenty-four books a year help her to be an expert in her field by staying current with business trends.

Attend training and conferences. Training programs and conferences can be great opportunities to learn. In growth economies today, there are many programs offered to women by organizations such as businesswomen's organizations, institutions of higher learning and government or nongovernmental entities.

Daniela Martin is Director of Management at AmCham Argentina, a chapter of the American Chamber of Commerce. This fast-talking, fast-moving, bottom-line-oriented, intense young woman has effectively managed a series of promotions during her tenure at AmCham. She started as an intern and today is managing other staff members. What's the secret to her success? Results. Daniela knows that having the expertise to deliver results is so important that she negotiated an agreement with her boss wherein AmCham gives her an entire month off every year to continue to further develop her skills. Each year, Daniela and her boss determine what type of development she most needs. She researches various options and then either finds the funding for the development opportunity or pays for it herself.

Indian writer and entrepreneur Ritika Bajaj also makes developing her expertise a habit. "I have always believed in continuous professional development. I've kept abreast of new ideas and trends in my industry, as well as in others. I have reinvented myself when needed, moving from one medium to another. I have also continued to learn through whichever avenues were available to me. I network with people from all walks of life and attend professional development forums that are relevant to my line of work. I honestly don't know where I want to get to or if I am there yet, but the way I do it is by religiously sitting and contributing in some way every day to myself and my work. Growth, both professionally and personally, is a daily activity," she said, concluding, "I find connection and meaning in the work I do and I stay in touch with those I work with, not leaving any room for miscommunication. I truly believe that the only way you can get ahead in your career is if you take everyone along with you. Careers are not made in isolation; several people contribute to your success."

NOW IT'S YOUR TURN

To continually expand and deepen your competence, get the job experience and build the skills that will help you the most. On-the-job, hands-on experience is usually the best way to learn. Training is the right learning option if you need to develop a new skill that you cannot readily acquire at work. Reading is most valuable when you want to broaden your base of knowledge. Feedback is most useful when you have the skill you need, but need to improve it.

If you work at a company that provides regular training opportunities, you are fortunate and should take full advantage of what is available. If you don't have such opportunities and you need to identify training opportunities in the marketplace, do some research before you sign up for a program. First, identify the competency you want to develop, and how you intend to use what you learn in your job or future jobs. Then evaluate programs for how effectively they meet your needs. Research the caliber and experience of the organization and the trainer providing the training. If you are able, get a recommendation from someone who has attended the program or other similar programs.

ACTIONS TO DEVELOP COMPETENCE

Use the following three steps to develop a plan to increase your competencies.

1. Review your notes from the action section of Chapter 2 to evaluate your areas of strength (see page 82). Remember, the purpose of that exercise was to identify the skills you do well. Pick your two top strengths.

2. Pick two areas of knowledge or skill that you want to develop further. These can be areas of weakness or skills you think will be important to your career in the future.

3. Using the four methods of learning discussed in this chapter (learning from experience, feedback, reading, and attending training programs) build a learning plan for the four skills you identified in Step 1 and Step 2 above. (See the Sample Learning Plan on the next two pages.)

SAMPLE LEARNING PLAN

SKILL	EXPERIENCE	FEEDBACK
Strength 1: Finance	Ask to take on additional financial responsibilities at work by X date	
Strength 2: Business Development	Implement two new sales techniques by year's end.	Go on three difficult or challenging customer calls with more experienced salespeople by X date.
New Area 1: Social Media		
New Area 2: Mobile Tech		Ask questions about how people use mobile technology

READING	TRAINING/CONFERENCE
	Identify and attend a training program in advanced selling techniques.
Do some online research on best ways to leverage social media every week.	
Read about developments in the mobile space once a month.	

SUMMARY

To prepare for success, it is important to build a strong base of business knowledge and regularly hone your skills. Being highly competent is one way to overcome certain obstacles.

Everyone is busy, and it's easy to decide that you don't have the time for learning and professional development—or to assume that you will be able to make time to study later. But putting off regular learning and professional development is a mistake. The foundation for a successful career is built on continually renewing a strong base of up-to-date knowledge and skills. Maintaining this strong foundation is one of the best investments you will ever make in yourself and your future. Make a plan to regularly develop the competencies you need to achieve your career or business goals.

NOTES

GET

SET

— HABIT 3 —

Focus

Your goals are the cues, your actions are your routines,
and your definition of success your reward.

WHEN YOUR DREAMS, YOUR GOALS, AND YOUR strengths align with what you do, how you live, and who you want to be, you will find contentment.

Don't let anyone ever tell you that you cannot achieve this alignment. It is yours to define and achieve. This alignment requires focus, a habit that includes regular introspection, intention, commitment, concentration, and, as always, action. The result of defining then creating the life that works best for you is real contentment and deep fulfillment.

A former American client of mine, Wendy Warner, holds a doctorate in analytical chemistry. Not surprisingly, she derived a formula for the habit of focus. It goes like this:

Focus + Belief Turns Possibility into Reality
$$F + B = P^R$$

If you can visualize what you want and believe you have what it takes to make your vision a reality, then you have the power and confidence to make your dreams come true. Focus is first about determining what you want. See the life you want in your mind's eye and imagine the contentment it would bring you. Go after it without hesitation.

THE FOUR STEPS OF FOCUS

Undeterred women regularly ask themselves these four questions.
1. Why? Why do I want this success (my reward)?
2. What? What are the specific goals I need to set to achieve my success?
3. How? How will I achieve these goals and what I want?
4. So what? Do I see results, and am I satisfied?

Visually, the cycle looks like this.

At its deepest level, focus is about determining what success looks like for you. What will be the source of the joy, meaning, and contentment that you want to experience through your work and personal life? Focus on this level is about determining your overall life purpose and the road you want to be on.

On the next level, focus is straightforward. You set specific goals to achieve what you want. Once your goals are set, focus is a matter of execution, of working steadfastly and tenaciously. At this stage, focus is about action. Concentrate on doing only what's most important. Don't let yourself get distracted by activities, people, or anything else that pulls your attention away from what you want to accomplish.

Last, focus is about regularly evaluating your progress and results. Check in with yourself at regular intervals to find out if you still want to achieve the goals you set in the past. Has your definition of success changed? Are you achieving what you set out to achieve? Why or why not? Are the goals you set actually getting you closer to your definition of success?

People who study and work on habits explain them as loops comprised of three parts: the *cue*, also called a trigger; the *routine*, actual behaviors or actions; and the *reward*, the payoff desired from those actions.[1] In terms of making focus a habit, see your goals as cues, your actions as the routine, and your definition of success as the reward. As with all the other success habits, focus is not a one-time process.

Let's now explore focus in detail, starting with your personal definition of success.

DEFINE
YOUR
SUCCESS

CHAPTER 5

CHOOSE

Success is finding personal meaning
and contentment in your life.

WHEN I REACH OUT TO A WOMAN FOR AN interview, I often get the same response, "Why would you want to interview me? I am not that successful." In each case, I ask the woman if she is doing what she wants to be doing at the moment and if she is happy doing it. Is she content with her life? In every case, they answer yes. So I respond, "You are just the type of woman I am looking for. You meet the definition of success that I use."

Society tells us that success means having the highest job in a company, wealth, and power. There are countless lists and articles on the world's "most powerful" or "richest" women, and as a result, we've bought into a set of hard-to-achieve ideals— just as we have bought into hard-to-achieve ideals for beauty, body, and family. We are regularly admonished for not scaling our businesses larger or not getting to the highest levels of corporations. We are constantly told what we should want or should do.

You and I know better. We know that we don't need to strive for anyone else's ideals and goals. Here's how Crystal Yi Wang talked about expectations of her. "When I was young, my parents borrowed a lot of money and sent me to learn piano, but I didn't succeed at it. My parents then sent me to learn English, hoping that one day I would go abroad with a scholarship for education, just like one of my cousins had, but I didn't excel at that either. In my early life, before my graduation from university, I never succeeded by my parents' standards. I was just a normal girl, who was never at the top of my class or the best in my family. I was always living in the shadow of my good friends and my cousins. I didn't realize the secret recipe of success until I started my first job. My dream career path was to work for a so-called Big Four consulting firm, but I wasn't even able to get an interview with one, so I decided to find a similar job working for any brand-name company. I planned that one day I would get an MBA so I could enter a professional services firm. My career grew from that first job I took. In ten years I went from being an assistant merchandiser at Wal-Mart to an associate director at Deloitte Financial Advisory Services. During that period I learned that I love consulting and that I believe it should be my lifetime career. Finding a job that I love is the luckiest thing that has happened in my life. My salary has increased thirty times since my first job in Wal-Mart."

We don't need to measure ourselves against another woman's desires and achievements. When we are true to ourselves, then our lives and our happiness are based on what we actually want, not on what others tell us we should want.

In the beginning, bold, charismatic Argentinian fragrance entrepreneur Marta Harff's definition of success was "to survive, to earn, to have tranquility, to help my family, to have a good life. I wanted to make money—I say that without shame. I have no fear about hard work, I don't know any other way." As she made money and was able to help her family and have the life she envisioned for herself, she defined the next level of success for herself, and this was to grow her business to a certain size. She has redefined her success several times in over forty years of working.

Define your success based on what you want to achieve and why you want to achieve it. Your definition of success is linked to the work you have already done to identify what motivates you. You can think of it as the reward you want for all your hard work, and the outcome you want to have when you implement the habits of undeterred women. You'll know you are successful when you feel fulfilled and content.

This is why the first aspect of focus that I want to introduce you to is how you determine and choose what success looks like for you: the reward you get at the end. Before you can concentrate on the actions of becoming successful, you have to figure out why you even want success. Your personal definition of success is the long-term payoff you will get for all the work you are going to do in the days, weeks, months, and years ahead. When you focus on your own success goals, you will feel in control of your actions and plans.

You may already know what you want in your career or business, and what you want your professional path to be. It may be as easy for you as it was for Renata Pessoa, Dr. Shahira Loza Doss, and Nour Jarrar. For them, the process of defining their success was rather straightforward. Renata Pessoa, Managing Director of Accenture in Brazil, shared, "I consider it a privilege to know what I want and to get what I want in my professional life." When Egyptian physician and entrepreneur, Shahira Loza Doss, M.D., who founded the Cairo Center for Sleep Disorders, spoke about the path to success, she said, "It's simple: Find your passion, set a goal, and persevere."

One of the most ambitious and forthright women I interviewed during my research on undeterred women is Nour Jarrar, a highly focused young woman who at the time of our meeting had already become Executive Manager of Strategic Planning for the Arab Banking Corporation in Jordan. Nour told me she had set her sights on becoming a bank CEO. She described her success in very vivid terms and told me about each of the positions she would have to perform well in to become a CEO. Nour is so career minded that on her twentieth birthday she asked family and friends only to give her presents that were items she could use at work.

Your version of success may or may not be easy for you to define. You may be the type of person who is not sure which professional direction to take, or even if you want to follow a career path. Perhaps like Chinese entrepreneur Liheng Bai, who started a company to counsel students entering college and to advise schools building counseling programs, your career journey thus far has included a series of trial and error discoveries or some detours along the way. Liheng shared, "I made many mistakes in my career. I think deep down we know what we are good at and what our hearts are calling us to do. I think I wasted my time—going into finance was a waste. It wasn't worth my time. I was always passionate about education, so I should have gotten involved in education a long time ago. When I entered the educational field, I realized how many different jobs there are in one industry! Now, I encourage students to follow their hearts. Once you figure out what you're passionate about in one area, such as advertising or finance, take time to see what you want to focus on." I think Liheng will ultimately find that her experience in finance was not a waste. Someday her financial knowledge will prove invaluable to her in managing the financial aspects and growth of her company.

Your career path may even feel like you've been on a trampoline jumping from one job, project, or assignment to another. Or maybe your career path is being slowly revealed to you with each position you take. Regardless of which of these most accurately describes your professional experience, having focus will give you clarity about the path to take next.

WAYS TO DEFINE SUCCESS

The best ways for you to determine your own definition of success are to:

Focus on what you are passionate about. Your passion relates to the motivators you identified in Chapter 3 (see page 110).

Rosa Maria Marte, founder of Green Art Market in the Dominican Republic, says: "The key to having a successful business is to love what you do. Every project you build will require time and effort, along with specific knowledge and skills. It will take risks and commitment. If you don't love what you do, it can be frustrating and both time consuming and money consuming."

Tala Badri, Founder and Executive Director of Centre for Musical Arts, in Dubai, who was named Emirati Entrepreneur of the Year in 2010, gave a TEDx talk in which she said: "My life is rich. It's no longer measured in stuff and titles like it used to be. I am a happier person because of it. I make a difference, whether it's to my daughter or my son, whether it's to the students I teach an instrument to, whether it's to the community that I bring a music service to, whether it's to my country—where I am actually contributing to its cultural growth and development. I am making a difference through music."[1]

Focus on objectives that you find meaningful. Pooja Goyal, co-founder of Intellitots, an Indian company that creates innovative learning-oriented programs and products for children ages six months to six years, talked about how she and her business partner, Shivani Kapoor, determined their sense of purpose. "We had both reached a point in our careers where we wanted to pursue a course where we could have significant impact. The education industry offered us that platform. We were both convinced of the importance of the early years and interested in the impact these years have on the child as an individual, on the family as a unit, and on society at large. Every small interaction we have with a child offers us an opportunity to make a difference."

She continued, "The desire to find meaning in what we do was definitely the biggest impetus behind Intellitots. In a nutshell, the primary motivating factor for me to become an entrepreneur was to move from success to *significance*. After having spent long years in the corporate world, I was soul searching to identify what I was passionate about."

Focus on what you want, not on what other women want. I'll never forget this conversation I had with a friend. I was sitting outside her house on the stairs leading up to her front door and sobbing. My son was seven years old, and I had the opportunity to take a break in my career. But when I tried scaling back, it didn't make me happy at all. As I cried, I told my friend that I knew many women would love to be able to stay home with their children for a few years. Her response has stuck with me all these years, "You are not those women, you are Rania. It only matters what you want."

During the four years of my research, many women recounted how they were often asked why they didn't want what "other women want." In their questioners' minds, this meant having a desire to be a good wife and mother, one who stays at home. Most of the women I interviewed actually are great wives and mothers, and they love being at home. At the same time, they also want and love to be at work.

Focus on your own aspirations. Don't lower or minimize your professional aspirations because other women (or the men) around you don't share your aspirations. Part of what helped Chebet Ng'ok, a financial consultant in Nairobi, Kenya, choose to pursue what she wanted was the encouragement of the then chief financial officer of the Americas at JP Morgan Chase Bank. They met at a training session Chebet attended. Sensing hesitation from some of the women in attendance that day, the CFO said, "Hey, don't leave all the toys on the table. You deserve this, too." He wanted the women to understand that there were many fun, rewarding career opportunities available to them, ones they could aspire to.

Kenyan entrepreneur Christine Khasinah-Odero's goals for her business are big and bold: "To grow Supamamas to become the most extensive online information hub for moms. I would also like to see Supamamas have more events, especially in mentoring other women, implement more social projects, and qualify for a grant. This would include running mentorship programs for girls in high school and college and more visits to children's hospital wards, homes." (Note how specific Christine's goals are. We'll revisit this in the next chapter.)

Don't be deterred by parental or societal norms. Some parents, teachers, and schools pressure young women to pursue certain majors and specific jobs because they have defined these jobs as "appropriate" for women. Don't let the beliefs of others dictate what you want for yourself. You are the best judge of which career is best for you.

Irina Bullara in Brazil spoke openly about how there are very few conversations with young people in her country about what they want to do and why they want to do it. From her perspective, capable, smart, young university students are often encouraged to pursue higher-paying jobs in fields like finance when their true interests lie somewhere completely different. While Irina has done very well in her early corporate career, she has a lot of passion and ideas about social ventures that have more than a financial impact on society and community. Irina speculated that she would likely feel more fulfilled working at an organization with a broader mission. She wanted more for herself and for other women her age, something beyond the safe and traditional corporate jobs they had been encouraged by their parents or their university to pursue. I saw Irina's altruistic bent first hand. Prior to my arrival in Sao Paolo, she offered to help me in several ways. Among these, she offered to act as an interpreter for a couple of my interviews with women who did not speak English—even though those interviews were scheduled for the day before her wedding! As this book went to press, I heard from Irina that she had switched career paths and was now involved in early education, a field more aligned with her values and interests.

Focus on where you want to go, not on what's standing in your way. For several reasons, I didn't learn to drive until I was twenty-six and after I was married. My husband taught me how to drive—not something I recommend early in a marriage. The hardest driving maneuver for me was merging onto a busy highway. Looking from the merge lane over to the seemingly endless number of fast-moving cars coming toward me, I couldn't figure out how I could possibly work my way forward onto the highway until Lance, my husband, said to me, "Stop looking at the cars. Look at the spaces between the cars. Keep looking at the spaces until you mostly see space, then press on the gas pedal and accelerate on in. That will be your spot." Achieving what you want is like merging on a highway. Focus on the opportunities not the obstacles. When we start seeing the open spaces, we can find our way into them.

When I founded the online career advice platform TheWayWomenWork.com, I decided that we would focus on women's success habits, not on their struggles. Because undeterred women are solutions focused, my advice to you is: Don't blindly accept that you will experience the same obstacles other women have faced. See the pathways not the pitfalls. Although focusing on your own goals will provide a unique set of challenges, having your own definition of success will keep you from giving up.

DEFINING YOUR SUCCESS IS A JOURNEY

Many women in growth economies are not given the opportunity to build a career around their passions. Especially for women who don't have an education, the choices are limited. Women from very conservative families often are not given the opportunity to study or work. Furthermore, in some countries, students of both genders, males and females, are not given choices about the type of higher education they can pursue. If they graduate at the top of their classes at school or achieve high grades, they are told they must pursue career tracks like engineering or science. In most countries if they don't score highly enough, they are not allowed to enter programs for fields like medicine, even if this is what their hearts desire. As difficult as the roadblocks may be, many women remain undeterred despite them.

Shahira Fahmy, the Egyptian architect, was one of those women who were going to be channeled into something she did not want to do. Shahira did really well in high school and because of her good grades she got a scholarship to the American University of Cairo to study engineering, a track only made available to students with a high level of achievement. But Shahira grew up surrounded by art and design and was inspired to pursue a career in design. Her mother is an interior furniture designer. She has an aunt who is an architect and artist. Shahira loves to draw and was encouraged in her art by her grandfather. So she decided she was not going to go along with the system. When she appealed her case to the university she was told that top students don't study architecture, but she persisted and finally got her way.

In the end, Shahira studied architecture at the Faculty of Engineering at Cairo University. She graduated with honors and received a master's degree in architecture in 2004. Shahira founded her own architecture firm, Shahira H. Fahmy Architects. She self-assuredly told me over tapas at a trendy restaurant in Cairo, "I planned all this ten years ago."

Finding your passion and purpose is a journey that involves self-reflection and often several stops along the way. It is not something you can just sit down and come up with. Leila Rezaiguia defined a new version of success for herself. After seventeen years in corporate talent management, she lost her passion for working at a corporation. Her heart and soul were no longer in it. Because of this, she quit her job and took a few months off to travel and "soul search." During this period she reflected on what she truly wanted to do. When she returned home, she decided to move to Dubai and start her own business, Kompass, a career coaching company that would build on her professional area of expertise.

Here's how Crystal Yi Wang summed up her journey. "From a normal girl in China to an assistant in a giant global corporation, to an associate director in the largest professional services firm in the world, and now also to being a part-time owner of a small jewelry studio and a mom, I have learned to define success for myself."

NOW IT'S YOUR TURN

Pay attention to what energizes you, not just what you are good at. Trust your passions and intuition in this process of self-discovery. There's no need to rush the process.

SELF-REFLECTION:
IDENTIFY OPPORTUNITIES TO CONTRIBUTE

If you don't already know what success looks like for you, here are some questions to ponder and explore on your own or with loved ones in moments of quiet and peace. Think, dream, and talk about some or all of these questions. Pick the questions that resonate with you and make note of your responses.

- What is the real reason I am here?
  Examples: To make a difference in my community, for my family, or to be an example for my children.

- What do I stand for?
  Examples: Progress, change, truth, innovation, or women's rights.

- Who do I choose to be?
  Examples: An influential leader, a contributing member of my community, or a good mother.

- What evokes my intense interest and a desire to take action?
  Examples: The arts, fashion, technology, innovation, or legal matters.

- What is missing from my life right now?
  Examples: Independence or challenge.

- Why would I feel more complete with this missing piece?
  Examples: Because I would . . . feel a proud sense of accomplishment, know I had made a difference, have contributed to my family, feel more financially secure.

- What would I like to be doing that I am not doing?
  Examples: Working, running my own business, playing a senior role, or serving on a corporate or community board of directors.

- What would I feel really great about accomplishing?

- What would bring me joy, serenity, and fulfillment?

- What would bring me contentment?

The answers to these questions contain clues to help you define your success.

ACTIONS
TO CHOOSE YOUR SUCCESS

Once you have your answers to the questions above and you are clearer about what is important and meaningful to you, the next step is to envision your successful life. Here's how.

- Describe want you want your life to be like.
  Examples: I want to . . . have a career/business, make a lot of money (or be financially secure), be married, remain single, have children, not have children. I want my life to be busy or quiet, easy, challenging, and so on.

- Pinpoint the work you would enjoy that also enables you to have what you described in answers to the preceding questions.
  Examples: Holding a powerful leadership position in a large corporation, running my own business, working for

a small company where I can have a lot of responsibility, or being part of a team and not have too much individual responsibility.

- Identify the businesses or ways in which you could realize your professional passions. If you don't know where these types of opportunities exist, share your insights with the professionally minded people you know and ask for their input.
  Examples: I could achieve what I want and believe I would enjoy working at . . . a bank, a startup company, a multinational company, an environmentally conscious small business, a family-owned business; or by being a consultant or starting my own independent business.

Summon the courage to choose what is most important and fulfilling to you. Find the strength and voice to explain your choices and develop the will to pursue what you want.

SUMMARY

Define success in terms of the long-term rewards you would like to experience both in your career and in other areas of your life. This is going to be very personal. You don't need to strive to meet anyone else's expectations, ideals, or goals. Keep yourself from measuring your success against another woman's desires and achievements. If you are true to yourself, then your life and happiness will be based on what you actually want.

Choosing your own success involves self-reflection and inquiry. Base your vision of success on what you feel passionate about and on your authentic desires. Give your vision time to reveal itself. Remember, success is a journey, so how you define it is likely to change as you follow your path and evolve.

CREATE
YOUR
PLANS

CHAPTER 6

CREATE

"A goal without a plan is just a wish."
Proverb

NIGERIAN ENTREPRENEUR, ADESHOLA KOMOLAFE explained her view of goal setting. "I understand that success is a process. It doesn't just happen but happens only when you deliver consistently more than is expected of you. It must be cultivated. So from the outset, I set out to be successful. I knew where I was going. I knew how to get there." Adeshola's success process included what she described as a "combination of focus, planning, and motion," a process of never procrastinating and always following through on her plans. "I set a goal and work toward it."

As a teenager, Adeshola's audacious goals were to graduate at twenty-one, get a master's degree by twenty-two, and earn a doctorate by twenty-six. With the exception of a Ph.D., she achieved her educational goals. Adeshola uses the same process when it comes to her business, Media Insight, an integrated marketing communications firm. Adeshola observed that Nigerian businesses were not offering effective brand messaging and did not realize that social media had become an important communications channel. She knew that she had the competence, confidence, and courage it took to take advantage of this gap in the marketplace. She said, "I had the competencies I needed, and understood the opportunity instinctively. I knew that communication had become a niche to take advantage of. The rest is history. I knew it was time to get into the market and run my own company. I knew that once I started there would be no going back."

Adeshola described accomplishing what you want as a "mindset of psyching yourself up to achieve targets, and relying on the people you admire and great leaders from industry to inspire you. It's a cocktail," she explained.

When I talk about creating a plan and goal-setting with younger women who are recent college graduates, I often get blank stares and some pushback to my comments. They say things like, "I don't know what I want. Things change so quickly and new opportunities arise, so how can I know what the future will bring?" or "It's not like it was in your generation, when careers were more straightforward."

I'll tell you what I tell them: *You don't need to have a whole life/career plan mapped out.* But having a plan and setting specific milestones will move you forward professionally. Careers and business success do not just happen. You'll need to manage your career or business progression proactively. To create your success plan, begin with your aspirations and desires to accomplish something specific. Don't worry if your vision and goals change once you begin to pursue them. What's important is to be deliberate in your thinking and planning. Be intentional and specific with your plans.

In India, a group of young women are doing just that. A 2013 survey of single Indian women aged eighteen to twenty-six, conducted by Women's Web, an online magazine, and CareerBuilder, showed that even in high-growth and changing markets, some young women who are soon to enter the workforce are already clear on what their career aspirations are. Thirty-five percent of respondents agreed with the statement, "I know exactly what I want to do," while 55 percent had "identified certain career options." Only a handful of women surveyed were undecided. The majority of the survey's respondents (70 percent) viewed themselves as "highly" or "extremely" career oriented.[1]

THE POWER OF CREATING A PLAN

You don't need to set lifetime goals, or even long-term goals, to be successful, although you certainly can have them if you know what they are.

Azza Fawzi, an Egyptian who during the time of our interview worked in Doha, Qatar, attributes her career success largely to the fact that she knows what she wants and how to get there, so she can set specific goals to do so. Azza has achieved consistent career progression at Royal Dutch Shell. She started as a financial controller and was subsequently promoted to a finance manager, and then again to a regional role covering the Persian Gulf. In Qatar, she was Vice President, Finance, for Qatar Shell GTL Limited. As she rose through the ranks of Shell, Azza identified each position she needed to take and figured out what she would need to contribute in each of the roles. Today, she is one of very few executive-level women working in her company and has significant responsibilities for some of the most important assets in Shell's portfolio.

Lyubov Simonova, the principal at Almaz Capital Partners, a major international technology venture capital firm in Russia has had clear objectives. "From early childhood, I have had the endpoint in my head," she said.

Most people find it easier to start with a few specific short-term goals about the type of job, the level of responsibility, or the amount of money they want. Others set goals to either start or grow a business. Salwa Bamieh, Director and Partner at MMIS Management Consultants in Amman, Jordan, set a goal to start a business. Salwa succeeded in starting her own company in spite of difficulty raising capital as a single woman—an experience that many women across the globe, even in developed western countries, also have.

Your goals will keep evolving. As they do, the goal-setting process will help you to stay focused and gain forward momentum. To make the best progress, use your definition of success as your guide, and keep your current career and life aspirations top of mind. Without a mental picture of your success and specific goals, you may be more susceptible to inertia and could flounder around without a sense of direction and purpose.

Set goals after you are clear on what's most important to you and what you want both in business and life. Many people set goals. What distinguishes the most successful people is how strongly they feel about their goals and the specificity of the goals they set.

Throughout my career, I have set many different professional goals. The first of these was to rise to a senior leadership position at Bank of America. I got to that position by accomplishing a series of specific goals. These included successfully completing the bank's management training program, working as an international banker, taking on staff roles, and managing people while making sure I was contributing to the bank.

My second major professional objective was to start and grow an independent business coaching practice. I set specific goals for what types of clients I wanted to work with, what kind of work I wanted to do, and I set specific revenue targets.

Today, my primary goal is to accelerate the success of at least 100,000 women like you. My tactics for this include writing and distributing this book, reaching women from emerging economies online and in person through speaking engagements, and writing career articles for the blog on TheWayWomenWork. com and other publications. I have learned that the more specific my goals are, the more likely I am to reach them.

Maja Jelisic Cooper, an entrepreneur from Croatia, a cofounder and major shareholder of Televizija Classicum Limited, a cable television company, also advocates setting specific goals. "When setting your goals, keep in mind that they should be realistic and doable, but at the same time ambitious enough to get you where you would like to be. It is important that you can quantify your goals and measure the results. For example, if you would like to increase your revenue, set a percentage or dollar goal, and a time by which you would like to do so. Let's say you would like to increase your revenue by 30 percent by the end of the fiscal year. You can do the same thing either by cutting costs or through expansion to XY markets."

She continued, "I try to set my goals by using the SMART principle: making them *specific, measurable, accountable, realistic,* and *time-defined.* In this case, creating a budget and each month checking projected and actual figures against it would make your goals measurable and force you to keep a close eye on your progress. This will also enable you to make adjustments as needed and to keep pushing yourself and your team to achieve your goals."

BE PREPARED FOR PLAN B

Although your goals will guide you, you should be prepared for your plan not to work out. The career trajectory of Turkish entrepreneur Melek Pulatkonak is a great example of the twists and turns that careers can take. At the time of our interview, Melek worked for Microsoft. She is also the cofounder of

Turkish WIN, a networking platform for women with familial, cultural, or professional ties to Turkey. Her guiding philosophy is: "Always set goals and targets, but be open to the very different ways those goals might be achieved. If plan A doesn't work, there will be a better plan." That's been Melek's experience.

Melek's academic goal was to get a doctorate in gender studies so that she could implement economic policies in Turkey that would make a difference for women. But she was unable to get the scholarship she needed to pursue the Ph.D. Since that was her plan A and she didn't have a plan B yet, she wasn't sure what she'd do next. She decided to bide time before reapplying for a scholarship. With a little money from her parents, she went to New York City and lived with an aunt. She knew she had to find a job or she would not be able to afford to stay for long. Since she had no network or contacts, she went to a public library and scoured the job listings in *The New York Times* looking for any economics research jobs she could find. She applied for all the research associate positions that were available. Against the odds, she was offered a job at the New York Stock Exchange (NYSE).

Melek thought she would only work at the NYSE until a scholarship opportunity for the degree she wanted materialized. It never did. After three years at the NYSE, she leveraged her experience to get a job back home in Turkey as an advisor to the chairman of the Turkish Stock Exchange. But the attitude of the men on the exchange, her reflection back upon how difficult it was for women at the NYSE, and her perception that women who were getting ahead in finance had to look and act like men, led her to conclude that this, too, was not the right plan for her.

Melek determined that what would help her career plans was more competence especially in business. So she applied for and was accepted in the master's program in business administration at Columbia Business School. After graduating with her MBA, she landed a job at a tech startup company in New York City, where she worked for seven years.

Then one day, at an innovation conference, she happened to be standing in line next to the general manager of Microsoft in Turkey. Hearing him speak Turkish to someone else, she struck up a conversation. He was so impressed with Melek that right on the spot he asked her to join the Microsoft team in Turkey. Armed with great work and educational experience, Melek had a new plan and she headed back home to Turkey once again.

WAYS TO CREATE A PLAN

Just setting goals is not enough. As we discussed in Chapter 3, you have to have the motivation, initiative, and courage to stay on track to achieve success. The probability that you will achieve your goals increases with each of the following steps you take.

1. Set an intention to achieve your goals.
2. Decide when you will achieve your goals.
3. Create a plan to achieve your goals. It is very important to determine the first step you will take and when (the date, time, and place) you will take it.

4. Commit to someone (your boss, a peer, a friend, a mentor) that you will achieve your goals.

5. Last, and most important, to increase the probability of meeting your goals dramatically, set up specific and regular appointments with someone to whom you feel accountable for achieving the goals you set. Select someone who motivates you, whose opinions you value and who will encourage you but will be tough with you if you are not on track. For an example of this strategy in action, we need look no further than to people who exercise with trainers. This last factor is the reason why so many successful business leaders around the world have coaches like me with whom they regularly meet.

I've seen how effective taking these steps is from three different perspectives: throughout my years managing people at Bank of America, in my consulting business, and now at the Way Women Work. At the bank, I saw that when I set up a specific time to review my employees' professional goals, it increased the likelihood that they would attain their career aspirations. As an executive business coach, I find that my clients accomplish their goals when we hold regular meetings to review their personal definitions of success and their goals. In my own business, the Way Women Work, I meet regularly with and feel accountable to Erin Risner, my teammate and our Director of Community Engagement. These sessions have made a significant positive impact on our results.

Finally, I know unequivocally that if I had not had regular meetings with Ishita Gupta, my writing coach, and then with Stephanie Gunning, my editor, I never would have completed this book, nor would it have turned out the way it did.

This is how Taisiya Kudashkina, cofounder and CEO of Tulp.ru, the leading Russian review website for local businesses, achieves her goals. "I meticulously list everything that I dream of accomplishing and make a promise to myself to take one step a day toward my dreams. One step a day. I open up the list and take one little, tiny, wee step a day. Just a little call. Just a small conversation. Just one slide for the presentation. Using this approach, I raised three million dollars for my own startup and was able to surround myself with the best people, the brightest team. I am pursuing my dream. There are still lots of desires unfulfilled, but I am definitely enjoying the journey."

STAY ON TRACK: CONCENTRATE

Like most people in the world, you likely will not achieve all your goals. Many will be difficult. Some will be unattainable. No matter how hard they are, you will be more successful if you concentrate on your goals and plans. Don't get distracted by irrelevant or easier tasks, and don't get caught up in activities that won't help you reach your goal. Distractions could be anything from meaningless meetings to events where you are not connecting with the right people, or working on tasks that are unimportant. In coaching executives, I have found that the most successful ones have an unrelenting focus on their most important priorities. They don't let unimportant tasks crowd their days or cause them to work lots of hours. Instead, they concentrate on doing what they know will tie in most directly to their success.

Be confident that you have developed a good plan. Then work your plan and summon the courage to take the tough actions necessary to accomplish what you have set out to achieve. Notice that once again, we have cycled back to the need to be courageous in order to move forward in spite of any fears.

Born from her two passions, film and technology, Celeste North founded NuFlick in 2011, a website for on-demand alternative and indie films for the Latin American market. During a conversation, Celeste shared, "Some days it's very difficult to balance all of it, but I'm passionate about my startup and about inspiring others to create their own companies. NuFlick, in general, has been a huge challenge and it has taken all my courage to start it and stay with it."

Celeste continued, "Like all startups, some days you're up and some others you're down. The challenge is never to lose focus and to strike a balance between work and having time for yourself. You need to remember why you are the right person to solve the problem and to concentrate on your passion for your company. It's a challenge every day."

When our goals are challenging, we have a tendency to turn our attention back to what's easy and familiar—our comfort zone, the place where we don't encounter fear and resistance. I can't tell you how many times I wanted to give up on writing this book. Writing it was difficult and challenging for me in so many ways that I was often tempted to go back to doing what I have been very successful doing: business coaching. But you kept me from giving in to that temptation. Since my definition of success is to positively affect the professional lives of women in growth economies, I just could not give up. When I felt that I was in danger of quitting, I would simply concentrate on my reason for writing and it would give me the drive I needed to overcome my fears and frustration. When Adeshola spoke with me about why she set out to be successful, she said, "The idea of failure is so uninviting and so costly that you simply tell yourself there is no alternative to success."

In this same way, undeterred women are not easily dissuaded. They persevere in spite of the difficulties. They stay focused on what they set out to achieve. I often tell my clients (and myself) that the hardest step is not the first one, for at the beginning of a journey you are excited, fresh, and ready to start. The last step is also not the hardest, because you can see the finish line and your goal is in sight. The middle steps are the hardest. In the middle, you have nothing but your motivation and resolution.

Staying on track is achieved through:
- Discipline.
- Managing your daily schedule.

When Estefany talked about her ability to focus, she traced this skill back to her days in the dance studio. "I have to say, ballet gave me discipline." After graduating from the National School of Dance in the Dominican Republic in 2009, Estefany would sometimes help her dad at his thirty-year-old company. Unexpectedly she fell in love with the business. Without regret, she quit dancing in 2010 to become General Manager of A.M. Frutas y Vegetales SRL. "Dancing gave me the knowledge that if you want something, you really have to work for it; it is not going to fall from the sky. Everyone around me knows that when I want something, I have to get it, and I will work for it until I get it. It's about being inspired by what I do, being driven. Every day I feel like if I take a step—and it can be a small one, not a mile—then I'm achieving. Every day I work for it. I work really, really hard . . . and go for it. I'm not scared of getting what I want."

In Africa, Divine Ndhlukula, founder of SECURICO, a company with more than 3,400 employees and annual revenues of US$13 million dollars in Zimbabwe, found that the key to staying focused is how she organizes her schedule. She makes sure that her schedule first and foremost includes the actions that are most important, the ones that lead to the achievement of her goals and to her definition of success. Divine knew from a young age that she wanted to start her own business. Here's what she had to say about staying focused: "I have learned that the secret of success is found in one's daily schedule. My advice to women all the time is, 'If you want a certain future, go out, and create it. Conquer your fears, as fear is what enslaves most women.' Opportunities are now galore. We just need to roll up our sleeves, lift our feet, and walk through the door, as no one will carry us."[2]

Making time to restore yourself is one of the keys to maintaining discipline and managing your schedule. It may seem counterintuitive, but if you want to achieve better results, be more productive, and have more energy, then you should take breaks and daydream—even try taking short naps. The time away from your work is as important as the time doing your work. Regular breaks are rejuvenating and allow you to better solve problems, be more creative, and produce better results when you get back to work.

MEASURE YOUR PERSONAL SATISFACTION

When we adopt and stick to a habit, we do so because we want to achieve a certain reward or outcome. We work in vain if we continue to take action without checking back to see if we are actually creating the outcome we desire. It is also crucial to stop and evaluate whether or not we still want the outcome we began with. As Russian entrepreneur Taisiya said, "I have a repeated habit of stopping and making sure that everything I am doing right now is really what makes me happy."

As you set goals and take regular, consistent action to achieve what you define as success, I highly recommend that you continually assess your actions to see if they are producing the outcomes you originally envisioned. Many people never stop to make this evaluation. They keep taking actions they developed even when those actions are not producing results. In fact, some people confuse activity and results. The reason for your actions should be to achieve an outcome, not just to engage in activity for activity's sake.

You likely won't achieve all the goals that you set—nobody does. Also just as likely, you may no longer want to achieve some of the goals you originally set. Be prepared for these moments. They are inevitable. As you encounter failure, remind yourself of its inevitability. Think instead about how you are building self-confidence from being realistic about your capabilities and how your goals are taking you beyond what you achieved in the past. As Maha Al-Ghunaim, founder of Global Investment House, a Kuwait-based financial firm, said, "When you are climbing the ladder, you have to balance between speed and safety."[3]

NOW IT'S YOUR TURN

The Hindu concept of *dharma* has a complex meaning that's impossible to convey without context. In essence, it relates to a person's "right way of living," which encompasses their actions, duty, and vocation. As you define and redefine your personal definition of success, create a plan, set and reset goals, meet some goals, and miss others, you will continue to approach the vision of what's right for you.

SELF-REFLECTION: YOUR GOALS

With your definition of success in mind, ask yourself these questions:

- Do I know what it will take to achieve what I want? *Examples: Time, money, contacts, or other resources.*

- Am I underestimating what I need to do and how hard it might be?

- Am I prepared to achieve the professional or business goals I want? If not, what knowledge or skills do I need? *Examples: Financial skills, sales skills, or technical skills.*

- What do I already know and have achieved that will give me the foundation to achieve success? *Examples: A strong referral network. Prior similar types of achievements. Access to funds.*

- What has already helped me get to where I am today? *Examples: My expertise in X. My contacts with Y. My reputation.*

- How much money and what type of support will it take for me to have the type of life I desire?

Working through these questions will help you define and narrow the goals you need to set to achieve your definition of success.

 ## ACTIONS
TO ACHIEVE YOUR GOALS

Try using the following approach to set your goals. Imagine that you woke up tomorrow morning and found that you had achieved your definition of success! See yourself in that place. Visualize and feel what it would be like. Are you with me? Great!

Now, from that perspective, go back and think about the steps you took to arrive at this great place. Group the steps together into overall actions. Use these as the basis for your goals, and then take the following steps to set and achieve your goals.

1. Set three or four goals (no more) that you can reach over several months—a year at the most. These are the short-term goals that will eventually get you to your long-term reward, the realization of the vision that is your personal definition of success.

   - Ensure that these goals are very clear and specific, and include the date by which you want to achieve them.
     Examples: By July 20XX, I will get three new clients worth X in revenue. By September, I will attend a training session to learn how to X.
   - Contrary to what you may have been taught in the past, set goals that you believe you can achieve—goals that are within your reach.

2. Set an intention to meet your goals. Then:
   - Write down your goals.
   - Put them someplace visible, where you can regularly see and focus on them.
     Example: Write them on big notes and put them on the wall above your desk.
   - Share your goals with someone you trust and to whom you feel accountable.

3. Plan how you will achieve your goals.
   - Break down each goal into specific steps you (or someone else) need to take.

- Write down the first step you'll need to take for each goal and when and where (the date, time, and place) you'll take it.
- Schedule specific times on your calendar to work on your goals.

4. Review your progress and results.
   - Develop a system and schedule to review your progress. Spend time examining whether the actions you are taking are producing the outcomes you want, and whether or not you still want to achieve your original goals.
   Examples: Create a spreadsheet. Put the actions you intend to take in your calendar. Leave space beside them to track your impressions.
   - Set up regular appointments with someone to whom you feel accountable in order to review the goals you set.

Remember, it is critical to develop a schedule that works for you. Identify your most productive and creative times of day. Know when you prefer dealing with people versus working alone. As you build a specific schedule of days and times of day to work on certain priorities, set up specific appointments in your schedule. Stick to those dates and times just like you would any other important appointment. Do not allow people or unimportant tasks to encroach on the time you have set aside to work on your goals.

SUMMARY

Creating a career or business plan does not mean that you need to have your whole life mapped out. It means that you have a plan with targets and milestones that move you forward professionally. Begin with the desire to accomplish something specific. Start with your aspirations, even if they change once you begin to pursue them. From this intention, create a precise plan of short-term actions to take by a certain date and time. Plan out how you are going to accomplish each step. Find ways to stay on track, including reporting your progress to someone who will hold you accountable. Have confidence in your plan. Summon the courage to work your plan and to take the tough actions required to accomplish what you have set out to achieve.

Some goals are more difficult to accomplish than others. Keep a plan B in your back pocket in case your plan A is thwarted. Understand that you won't be successful in attaining your goals 100 percent of the time. Regularly assess your plan. If your plan isn't bringing personal satisfaction, begin the process again by evaluating what is important to you and setting a new plan in motion.

NOTES

— HABIT 4 —

Integrate

*"Career-only success is not success.
Success means success within yourself, with your family,
and in life, which includes your career."*

Nubia Correia

Brazilian corporate executive

I ASKED HAIFA DIA AL-ATTIA, CEO OF THE QUEEN Rania Foundation in Jordan, why she thinks so many educated women in the Middle East decide not to pursue a career. Among reasons that include insufficient public transportation, lack of public preschool programs, and familial or societal pressure on women to stay at home, Haifa also believes that women erroneously assume that they cannot successfully manage both their home lives and their careers. "Even though," as she said, "they have seen women airline pilots, CEOs, lawyers, and bankers—to name but a few of the jobs Jordanian women have—they don't think it is possible to have both."

Preparation and focus are the foundational success habits for undeterred businesswomen in emerging economies, but without figuring out how to integrate their work into the life they want for themselves, they would not be able to have a career or own a business.

NOT YOUR FATHER'S WORKPLACE

Work today is different from work two decades ago. You are different than women in your mother's generation. Opportunities in growth economies are different than opportunities available today elsewhere in the world. You have more resources and assistance available to you than women had in the past. You live in a different place and you are seeking career success at a different time. If you choose to do so, your mindset about your life and work can also be different.

Let's examine some of the differences, starting with what's happening in the workplace today. No longer does every job have to be done during regular business hours or in an office. Technology has enabled a completely different way of work. Even when they don't have formal policies, most employers will provide some flexibility to allow high-performing employees to meet their work-life demands.

There are more women in the workplace and more female managers and leaders than ever before. You can aspire confidently to become one of them. For that matter, no longer does everyone have to work for a company. There are women all over the world who are self-employed or starting their own businesses.

You are different. You are educated and confident, attributes that women who came before you may not have had.

Opportunities for you therefore are different from those that were available to them. You likely live in a place where there is a demand for skilled labor and for people with talents like yours. New jobs are created every day. You, yourself, may be someone who wants to create jobs. You may also live in a place where you have support from others capable of enabling you to have the type of life you want. The habit of integration is the way you structure or tweak your environment and your life to be able to have and do whatever you want.

Your workplace is not your father's workplace and you don't have to work in the same ways he did. You can create your own future, one that works for you. You can give up the old ideas that to win at work, you lose at life, and that to have a good home, well-raised children, or be personally satisfied, you cannot be highly successful at work.

We don't need to be defined by the workplace behaviors of our fathers, who gave much up at home to strive for success at work and to provide well for their families. Nor should we be defined by the example of the many mothers who felt no choice other than to sacrifice their career ambitions for their children, homes, and husbands.

SECOND SHIFT

I encountered one of these differences when I asked undeterred women about the tensions between their life and work priorities. I was taken off guard the first time a woman turned my line of questioning right back on me. It turned out not to be an isolated incident. I had similar conversations with many other women.

The conversations went like this. After I asked several questions in a row about work-life trade-offs, a woman would say something like, "I think western/American women have much worse work-life struggles than we do here."

"Why do you think that?" I'd ask.

She would respond by asking, "What do you and women like you have to do after work or on weekends?"

My answer: "In addition to spending time with our children, husbands or boyfriends, family, and friends, and engaging in activities we do for fun, we also have to go grocery shopping, cook, clean, and run numerous errands."

"Exactly!" the woman would say, and then she would use the following specific words: "Western women have 'second shift' much worse than we do here."

The first woman to share this perspective with me and use the term *second shift* in this manner was Maisa Batayneh. Maisa is the founder, sole owner, and principal architect at Maisam Architects and Engineers in Amman, Jordan. When we spoke, she had fifty employees and a second branch of her business in Abu Dhabi. At the time of our interview her husband was the mayor of Amman. This meant that Maisa had many important priorities in her life: a family, a business, children, and many community responsibilities as the wife of a political leader. Although I was already familiar with the concept, I asked Maisa what she meant by it. She described *second shift* the same way I do, as the household chores and primary responsibility for the day-to-day care of the children or elderly parents that working women have before and after work.

Many women in growth economies have a lighter second shift than their western counterparts. In their communities and perhaps in yours, extended family takes a more active, hands-on role in raising children. People live in neighborhoods with family close by, and in some cases their extended family members even live with them. For middle-class or higher-income families, domestic help for household chores is reasonably affordable and common.

Economist Qian Liu, Ph.D., in China, astutely compared women in the United States, China, and the Scandinavian countries. "Finding balance between family and work is very difficult everywhere. It's easier for professional women in China, as women have their families' support with child care. One can turn to parents or grandparents to bring up the kids and share part of the housework, which makes working women's work-life balance a lot easier. Hiring a nanny in Asia is also much cheaper than in the United States or Europe. Nordic countries support families with a lot of subsidies. In Sweden, for instance, parents have eighteen months of parental leave, and the government's child care program is of great quality, too. If you look at the statistics, it's not about whether women can or cannot have it all. It is more about women and men allocating their resources more efficiently; investing their time, efforts, and resources in their work, family, and children."

Support from family, friends, and servants helps decrease many of the pressures women face at home. If they choose to have careers, it enables women to put more energy into achieving success at work. Many of these same women, who welcome and value the support they receive from their families and domestic staff, wish more women in growth economies would take advantage of various forms of support to pursue a career or start a business.

Support in the second shift means having a leg up over other women, especially western women. Support in their second shift is part of the equation that enables many women to pursue higher levels of success at work.

A 2014 Grant Thornton survey of publicly traded and privately held companies conducted in forty-five countries, both advanced and growth economies, found that the United States had the lowest percentages of women in senior management. By contrast, Eastern Europe, Southeast Asia, and China, places where women have easier second shifts, have the highest percentage of women in senior roles.[1] Russia, at 43 percent, ranked as the country with the highest percentage of women in senior management. Other top ten performing countries included the growth economies of Latvia, Thailand, and Philippines.[2]

WORK-LIFE INTEGRATION ON YOUR OWN TERMS

Integration of life and work is the toughest and most elusive of the six success habits that undeterred women in growth economies employ. For many women, their definition of success includes a quality of life most typically referred to as *work-life balance*. Sometimes, however, no matter how many plans and routines are put into place, arrangements fall apart. I'm sure you've had those days, too!

The often repeated questions of whether or not women can "have it all" and conversations about the sacrifices women have to make in order to have full home lives as well as careers are outdated. Like the prevailing metaphor of the glass ceiling and glass walls that women face in the workplace, these obsolete ideas do not actually govern what is or is not possible for any woman today.

Since there are billions of people in the world, there are just as many possible definitions of an ideal integrated life. The path to an integrated life therefore will be personal. What works for one woman may or may not work for you, me, or for anyone else. The habit of integration is the way a woman structures and customizes her environment and her life to choose what she wants.

At the heart of every woman's successful work-life integration is her ability to organize her life and career around her own values and definition of success, rather than basing her choices and activities on what others think. Work-life integration is not about implementing other people's values; it's about each woman implementing her own.

Regardless of the nature of their priorities, undeterred women in emerging economies share the view that work-life integration is attainable. They know, and prove by example every day, that it is possible to have successful careers despite their other life priorities. Furthermore, they take advantage of the changes in the modern workplace to create their integrated lives. Undeterred women are not governed by the past, by tradition, or by ideas of what women should or should not do and can or cannot do. They design their lifestyles to blend their office time with their personal lives, and their time at home with their work.

NOTES

INTEGRATE WORK INTO LIFE

CHAPTER 7

CUSTOMIZE

"There is no recipe, no secret handbook for how I manage work and life. It is this thing called living."

Gordana Frgačić

Croatian author and HR manager

I SAW ONE OF THE MOST FASCINATING EXAMPLES OF work-life integration and the changing role of women in the workplace during a meeting I held in Buenos Aires, Argentina, in November 2013. I met with twelve female entrepreneurs at NXTP Labs, the business accelerator cofounded by Marta Cruz. A business accelerator is a program that provides advice, guidance, support, and funding to help entrepreneurs get started with their business ideas. As I asked questions of the women, many of whom had not known each other prior to the meeting, I learned that nine were in business with their husbands. In all nine of these cases, the couples had either jointly founded the company or the husband had joined his wife in the business after she had grown it. In none of the cases had the wife joined the business to help her husband.

As the entrepreneurs spoke with me about their business plans and the business climate in Argentina, they also talked about how sharing a business with their husbands contributed significantly to their husband's understanding of their work demands. Sharing work responsibilities led these couples also to begin sharing household responsibilities.

Some undeterred women choose to prioritize their family. Others prioritize themselves and personal fulfillment. Others prioritize work. Still others have a dual focus on work and family. Any of these choices is wonderful if the choice is fulfilling to the individual. Women I spoke with span the entire gamut of women in the workforce. Many were mothers. Some were not. Many were married. Others were divorced or widowed. Many had supportive husbands. Some were shouldering their decisions to work on their own. Many had figured out how their children would be taken care of while they were at work. Some, in very emotional ways, shared that they had abortions because they could not figure out how to achieve the level of success they desired if they had more children. Some women had work-life integration figured out until something like the demands at home, extreme work hours, travel requirements, or stress led to a decision to leave the workplace. Each woman had to make individual decisions about her work and home life so she could pursue her personal definition of success.

THE PRESSURES OF MOTHERHOOD

Work-life challenges persist for women in growth economies as they do for women everywhere else. Sandra Portugal, an IT executive in Brazil, described her decision to spend more time with her family as the greatest risk she has ever taken in her career. She shared, "The riskiest thing I've done professionally was when I stepped down from the highest position in a company so that I could balance my career with the needs of my family. I made the right choice for myself despite it looking unwise in the eyes of my competitors."

In terms of making her own choices, Chinese journalist Zhen Wang who was expecting her first baby soon after our interview, spoke about making a decision many other women before her have made to, as she called it, "moderate her career ambitions." Nevertheless, she went on to say, "I will not become a stay-at-home mother, as this is boring. I am taking advice from many women. Overall, the journalism job is ideal for women in China, especially for young mothers. This is because we do not have fixed working hours. We do not have to go to the office every day."

For some women, there are times when having mutual success at work and at home seems unattainable, so they make a decision to leave the workplace. That's the tough decision that Xiomara (Xiomy) Ricardo had to make. Xiomy is originally from Mexico, but was living in Sao Paulo, Brazil, when we spoke. She had enjoyed a rewarding career as a manager at a multinational company. "People think it's a luxury not to have to work, but I have never felt that way." Xiomy had taken seven months of maternity leave (by most assessments, a very generous leave period) following the recent birth of her son. She asked the company to extend the leave even further, but they wouldn't do it. Now with three kids at home, she was struggling to figure out if she could or would go back to work.

Xiomy emotionally shared that she had defined so much of herself through her work that she didn't like the idea of not working. She wasn't sure what she would do. "There are no part-time jobs and no flexibility at most companies in Brazil," she said. While on maternity leave, Xiomy had discovered that she was extremely talented at decorating cakes and had been asked by several mothers to create themed cakes for their children's birthdays. As she showed me a picture of one of her truly unique cakes, which was shaped like a hamburger, she wondered out loud about the possibility of opening a cake shop.

Some mothers raise their children on their own and still figure out how to build their careers. In Rio de Janeiro, Brazil, Núbia Correia, an executive director at EY, emotionally shared her experience, "When my children were born, I was married. All my children have the same father, but we divorced when they were very young. My divorce was not easy and my relationship with my ex-husband was not good. Until now, we haven't been able to establish a friendship or hold an easy conversation. That meant that during my children's infancy and adolescence, at crucial points related to education, values, needs, and so on, I was alone taking care of them all the time, taking risks by myself, with parenting decisions 'splitting me' in twenty ways in order to accomplish all the tasks that were necessary. I had to take on different roles: sometimes I was the mother offering comfort or help with homework; sometimes the father making the rules and teaching discipline.

"I was responsible for working and meeting all my children's needs (food, clothing, shelter, school, and so on). Meanwhile I was a woman with my own needs, having to balance my needs with the needs of my children. I had support from a babysitter who has worked for me since 1997. She was a very important supporter for my children during challenging periods. I am very proud of those moments when I continued working, studying, looking for my place in the world, and advancing in my career at the same time I was a mother, educating my children with the best values I could."

She continued with pride, "When I was with my children, I was entirely with them, and I am sure that was a very important influence in regard to their ethical way of living. They are great human beings—honest, responsible, and studious. Looking back, I am sure there were things to change, there were better ways to accomplish the same results, but I did the best I could do with what I knew at the time. My children are the best of me that I can offer to this world."

OTHER MOTHERS DON'T FEEL PRESSURED

I interviewed many young women, especially ones in their late twenties and early thirties, who had a very different perspective about work-life challenges. In fact, they did not experience much tension at all in managing work and the rest of their lives. These women are very pragmatic and expressed little angst about how to fit work into their lives. They were comfortable with the arrangements they had made with their spouses, partners, child care providers, and places of employment. Paula Arregui, Product VP of MercadoPago in Argentina, who has been with the fast-growth company since its inception, for instance, was so comfortable that she answered email on her phone while she was giving birth in the hospital. Paula was controlled and calm when we met over appetizers in a trendy bar at the end of her work day. She said, "I love my kids, but it is also a pleasure to go to work!" When her baby was asleep in her arms, she would connect to the office and get on conference calls. She never said she felt pressure to do so from work, but rather that it was what she wanted to do. "It's 100 percent my decision. I am always thinking, 'What else can I do?' or 'How can I grow my career?'"

In 2012, Mwamvita Makamba had a career change that required a move from Tanzania, the country where she was born, went to school, and had always worked, to Johannesburg, South Africa. Away from the comfort of her family, she became, in her words, "officially a single working mum" to her then six-year-old daughter, Malaika. Her position as a business performance partner in corporate affairs for Vodacom International Business and a trustee at the Vodafone Foundation requires her frequently to be on planes and in hotel rooms in a different African country almost every week. She has managed to keep and integrate this schedule into her life.

Crystal Yi Wang spoke about a different type of challenge that some mothers in China face. "I am a new mother with a daughter who is only four months old. Luckily, I am still on my maternity leave. Being a working mother in China is not easy. My boss, a Canadian, told me that he thinks being a mother in China is much easier than in western countries because you can get a lot of help from your parents or hire a nanny. My answer to him was that this could be true, but sometimes your life is destroyed by having so many helpers. Because of the one-child policy in China, especially in Shanghai, there are two sets of grandparents and only one grandchild. So usually six or seven people (parents, two sets of grandparents, and sometimes a nanny) will surround that one kid to take care of her or him. Is it really necessary? My answer is NO. Many of my friends are devastated by needing to solve all kinds of arguments with their parents regarding how to raise their babies.

"My advice to other women is: Don't necessarily do what other people do. My husband and I decided to do something different. We hired a nanny and that's all we need. My daughter's grandparents are welcome to visit her once a week. Luckily, this turned out to be the right decision for us. My daughter is not spoiled. She is a very happy and self-regulated baby. She has slept peacefully through the night since she was two months old. Surprisingly, I have a lot of spare time during my maternity leave. Having a kid completes my life, but it does not occupy my whole life."

Gordana Frgačić of Croatia, an author, HR manager, gender-balance advocate, and mom of three, said, "When I want to shock people, I have two strategies. For the first one, I tell them that as a child I ate cooked chicken blood, which is a specialty in our region in Croatia. The second one is that I am a high-positioned working mother with two teenagers and a six-year-old."

When people learn this, they ask her, *"How do you manage it?"* According to Gordana, some people admire her, some can't hide their envy, some of them put on a face that reads, "Poor kids, poor husband," and some of them feel sorry for her or even think of her as a bad person. Gordana explained, "But of course, none of them knows anything about me; they just see what they want to see or what they think they see. They think that I am better or worse than they are, and the truth is that there are moments when I am really better and then again moments when I am really worse compared to them."

"When I am asked how I manage it, I feel obliged to give a smart and revealing answer that would help working women around the globe to catch up with their lives. But mostly I feel helpless because my answers are certainly not what they would expect. There is no recipe, no secret handbook for how I manage. It is just this thing called living."

I know of several women who prioritize work over family and like working long hours. I can also think of at least three instances when the managers of the women who were working long hours encouraged them to go home earlier. All three of these women are mothers. Their managers couldn't understand why the women would make the choice to work long hours on most days. In two of these cases, the women's companies hired me to see if I could (among several other things) persuade them to work fewer hours. But when I investigated the situation, the work schedule the women already had suited them, their children, and their husbands. While their long hours may not have seemed right to others, their schedules were right for them. They, their husbands, and their children were happy with the schedule the women currently kept. None of these women was uninvolved as a mother. None had a stay-at-home husband.

SINGLE WOMEN HAVE LIFE DEMANDS, TOO

Although the integration of work and life is most often discussed as it relates to working mothers, the challenge of balancing work with leisure, of course, does not apply solely to them. Every woman has life interests, pursuits, and obligations outside her career that are important to her. Single women and married women who don't have children get rightfully resentful when work-life integration issues are narrowly described to mean coping with the responsibilities of the workplace and childrearing. Many women have elder-care or parent-care responsibilities, husbands, and other relations and friends they want to spend time with. Women also have hundreds of interests and priorities, including exercise, pets, and travel.

WOMEN ENTREPRENEURS CREATE THEIR OWN ENVIRONMENTS

When some undeterred women find that corporate work environments don't accommodate their work-life needs, they create their own work environments that do. Around the world women start their own businesses, some prompted in part by the desire to have a more flexible and integrated life than many corporate environments allow. Indian women Parul Mittal and Ritu Uberoy both worked in corporate IT jobs for over a decade. They were ready for something new and different, and wanted more flexibility in their lives. In August 2011, they launched RivoKids.com, an online platform for parents and kids. Parul said, "I do most of my work from 8:30 AM to 3:30 PM while my kids are at school. I am very dedicated and motivated to be able to work from the comfort of my home. I set internal deadlines for myself and try my best to deliver on them. Evenings are mostly spent with family doing kids' homework, afterschool classes, and playing board games with intermittent work-related emails and phone calls. I typically like to keep my weekends completely work free with occasional exceptions now and then due to a deadline."

Ritu and Parul encourage women to believe they are as capable, if not more, than men, of doing a corporate job or running an independently owned business. "The key is not to give up your dreams. Often, the culture around them expects women to sacrifice their dreams to look after the young and the old in the family. Our advice to any woman is to take breaks when needed. Leave your job for a few months if required. But get back on the wagon soon enough. You deserve it, you need it, and it's better for the family in long run."

Another approach is the one taken by Sam Shiraishi, a forty-year-old mom of three children, entrepreneur, and well-known social-good blogger from Sao Paulo, Brazil. Sam unabashedly brought her beautiful, six-month-old daughter, Manuela, to our interview, as she did every workday regardless of whether she was going to be at the office or in a meeting.

When Sam gave birth to Manuela, she didn't want to stop working, but she also didn't want anyone else to care for Manuela. Sam decided to do something rather radical and include Manuela in everything she did. This was a different choice than she had made with her other children, sons then aged eleven and thirteen. When the boys were born, she had initially taken a year off and then had gone back to work. This time she wanted something different. Having a well-established, popular mom and family blog in Brazil gave her more courage about this decision because it fit with her focus and brand. She comfortably held and breast-fed Manuela, ate her own meal, and talked intensely and spiritedly about her experience. "At first I was afraid of what people would think when I brought Manuela with me everywhere," she said. "Now, I see that women are inspired by me. It's been very surprising and special. It is hard physically, but I am emotionally peaceful. I can breathe more easily."

Sam's style of work-life integration has influenced her business culture. Since she benefits from having so much flexibility with her own children, she provides similar flexibility for her employees. Her media company, Otagai Mídias Sociais, is set up to allow her employees who are parents, and people with physical disabilities, to work from home. One day a week, Sam even works part time. She says, "I see what I am doing as disrupting the model of the workplace. And even though not everyone is comfortable with this model, there are many people who trust me and want to work with me. A big issue for women in Brazil at work today is feeling they have to choose family or work. I wanted to create a new culture, a new habit."

According to Sam, although it is initially strange for many people when she brings Manuela to a meeting, after a while they reach out to hold and play with her daughter, and before long they don't seem to mind after all.

Another highly successful entrepreneur, Argentinian Maria Luisa Fulgueira, spoke about how she strives to be a role model for young women, "When I mentor young women, I invite them to my home for dinner to show them that they can have a family and be successful. This is a big concern of girls today, because they think they cannot have both. But I show them! I am an entrepreneur and a single mother with three kids. I want to keep working and be successful in work and life. To be a good mother, you have to have a support structure and delegate."

THE MINDSET OF INTEGRATION

What women tell me, what you would tell me, and what I know from my own experience is that in spite of numerous obstacles, undeterred women every day figure out the right formula for work-life integration.

Women who have the mindset of integration:

See work and life as compatible, not as opposite. They integrate rather than balance their work and personal lives. They see life in a multidimensional way, not as a scale that weighs two competing demands that constantly have to be balanced—and where one side outweighs the other and wins while the other side loses. They don't see life as a series of trade-offs, but rather as a combination. Their mindset is both/and, not either/or.

Customize their lives. They do not take a one-size-fits-all approach, nor are they influenced to imitate the lives that others lead. The type of life society thinks they should lead does not unduly influence them. Rather, they create a lifestyle that works for them, their families, and their jobs. They build a life that is the venue where they accomplish their definition of success. They can articulate what flexibility looks like for them on both the work and home front.

Dora Szwarc Hamaoui, Director of Novos Negocios at Fibra Experts in Sao Paulo, Brazil, has learned that for her, one of the best ways to integrate her family into her workday is to create a standing weekly lunch date with her sons. Every Wednesday, she blocks off several hours on her calendar and never takes another meeting that might interfere.

When it's lunchtime, she leaves her office and meets her sons at their grade school. It is a treasured appointment that they all look forward to and have come to rely on. "It is the highlight of my week!" she says. She also makes it a point to tell her sons about what she is doing at work. According to Dora, as her son was leaving for school that morning, before our interview, he encouraged her, "Good luck with your interview, Mom!"

Dora has to travel regularly for work, but has asked to reschedule when it interferes with her Wednesday lunch date—and guess what? Meetings and travel are usually easily rescheduled. She doesn't offer up the reason she can't meet unless she is asked specifically. Instead she says, "I have an important meeting I cannot miss at that time." She found it hard to say this at first, but since then has found people to be understanding and accommodating.

As Dora spoke about her solution, it was exciting to see her pride in how she developed this way of integrating her life and work. Her sons are proud of her and her important work, and being able to make them a priority in the midst of her workweek motivates her.

Don't agonize over work or life decisions. They don't turn the decisions that they make at work or at home into bigger issues than they are. If they are unable to do something with their children, they don't worry that it will leave a lifelong scar. If they cannot participate in something at work, they don't anguish that it will result in a permanent black mark on their record or interfere with their career progression.

Enlist help in enabling their integrated life. Undeterred women don't believe they're Superwoman. They value and rely on support from others to create lives that work for them. They pull together a support team on the home front that may include their husbands, their relations, their friends, and domestic help if they have access to it. They delegate at work or share responsibilities with their teammates. They don't try to do everything themselves.

Don't seek perfection. In the words of Aleksa Delsol, an illustrator from Mexico, "Done is better than perfect." The goal of perfection is one that plagues women around the world. One of the key messages that girls hear constantly is, "Be a good girl" and "do everything right." In order to have successfully integrated lives, we have to shift our sights from seeking perfection at home and at work to determining what will be enough to get the task done. We may even question if a task must get done at all. We have to figure out which things we need to excel at, and which we don't need to worry about.

Stop the guilt. Undeterred women minimize feelings of guilt about which parts of their lives are encroaching on the others. If they need to take care of something personal during "work hours," they figure out how to do so. If they need to take care of a work task during their "personal hours," they do so. They don't feel guilty about not being at home when they are at work and they don't feel guilty about not being at work when they are at home. They know that they are spending much more time at work than people have ever before in history, and that they are also spending more time at home with their families than people have ever spent.

During our interview in Doha, Reham Thawabi, an executive manager at Commercial Bank of Qatar, shared a conversation she had with her boss about the schedule she had established for herself and her family. Reham confidently and unapologetically told her boss, "Here's what I can do. I'll give you 100 percent from 7:15 AM to 5:00 PM every day. My children get my full attention from 7:00 PM to 9:00 PM each night. From 9:00 PM to bedtime is reserved for my husband and for me. On a normal, everyday basis that how it has to be for me to make work fit into my life. If there is an exceptional need in any one of these areas of my life, I will be flexible; and I expect my family and my employer to be flexible as well."

Know integration is a process. Women who seek an integrated life know that it is not always smooth sailing. What they, their families, and workplace put into place works sometimes, or for a while, or sometimes not at all. They are undeterred when they have to find new ways to have the life they want because they know they and their lives are worth it.

INTEGRATE, DON'T JUGGLE

During our interview, Vania Neves, Director of IT at a multinational corporation in Rio de Janeiro, Brazil, brought up an analogy first popularized in a commencement address in 1996 by the then-president and CEO of Coca-Cola Enterprises, Brian G. Dyson. He said, "Imagine life is a game in which you are juggling some five balls in the air. They are Work, Family,

Health, Friends, and Spirit, and you're keeping all of these in the air. You will soon understand that work is a rubber ball. If you drop it, it will bounce back. But the four others—Family, Health, Friends, and Spirit—are made of glass. If you drop one of these, it will be scuffed, nicked, damaged, even shattered. And it will never be the same."[1]

This imagery is powerful, meaningful, and has helped Vania and many others frame work in the right context in their lives. However, this metaphor perpetuates the notion that we are juggling, meaning we have to keep lots of balls in the air, that our mistakes are uncorrectable, and that we have to be skilled in our "juggling" act.

But that is simply not the case.

Women who most effectively manage their different priorities don't think about them as competing demands. They don't frame their decisions about work and life as either/or. Instead they think about what they want from their lives, and that includes their work. They think about ways to integrate their work more seamlessly into their lives; how they can blend aspects of their lives, not rotate between them. They think about what's important to them and seek ways to have all the important aspects of their lives, which include their careers, fit together. This may seem to you to just a different use of words, a semantic distinction. But it's not. It is a fundamental shift in mindset and behavior, a different way of thinking about a life that includes work.

When you blend or integrate aspects of your life, you think and act in a different way. Adopting the habit of integration frees you from worrying about potentially "dropping a ball." Life is not like juggling. You don't have to rush from one priority to the next, only keeping each in play long enough to toss it back up in the air before you have to move on to the next priority. You don't have to keep worrying that you are going to make a fatal mistake and drop the "glass balls," or even that when you drop the "rubber ball of work" you will look bad, like you don't know what you are doing.

Marketing director Michelle Wang from China shared her perspective. "The balance between being a successful professional woman and a good wife and mother has been a constant struggle for many women. Most men in China still have the perception that women should naturally take a bigger role in taking care of the family, so married women are less likely to take on more aggressive roles in business. I don't necessarily think the perception that women should take more responsibility for the family is wrong; in fact, I think there are quite strong biological and sociological reasons behind it. But I do think that in today's world, women should be given the opportunity and respect to make their own choices, and companies should develop more flexible programs for married women so that they don't have to give up one role or the other. After all, the loss of good female talent is a pity for today's business world."

Having a life that integrates work is all about making deeply personal choices. If you make the conscious decision to view your life as including a fulfilling career, although not being entirely defined by your work, then you will be on your way to making space for every aspect of your life that is important to you.

Gordana Frgačić asserted her perspective. "What is happening to you is normal and it's happening to women all around the world no matter if they are CEOs or bank clerks, saleswomen, or housewives. Not a single one of us has a unique formula for how to juggle and manage work and private life. It is very individual, and it depends on dozens of factors that sometimes you can, and sometimes you can't, influence. You just adopt the best possible way you can in order to make your life worth living."

She continued, "Don't allow shiny magazine covers to fool you and tell you that your life is totally worthless. Don't let your friends and neighbors make you feel small with stories about the great lives they have. If you are happy with your lot, it is the only thing that is important. Next time you hear somebody claiming women can or can't have it all, remember that they are just talking about their own lives, possibilities, and opportunities. You have all the right in the world to be angry. You have the right to be sad, to be silent, or talkative. You have the right to wear high heels, flat heels, to be tired, to have some fun, to stay in bed, to be a great or bad cook, to be skinny, or plus size. You have the right to postpone the project, to say no to your boss, to demand a higher salary, or to be satisfied with a non-managerial position. You have the right to have one, two, three, or more kids, or no kids; to be married or single; and to clean your house all day long if you want to, or to peacefully coexist with the dust in it. You have the right to earn less or more than your partner. You have the right not to take all the blame for bad sex in your partnership. You have the right to tell your partner, 'Get your ass out of your cave and help me, because I need your help now and not later when you are ready.' And you have the right to call all or any of these things your 'all.' So the best advice I can give you is that you have to decide for yourself what does having it all mean to you? What makes you happy and satisfied with your life?"

PUT YOURSELF AT THE CENTER OF YOUR LIFE

The habit of integration is developed by believing that you have enough time for the aspects of your life that you care the most about; that each has a space in your heart, mind, and schedule. Integrating your life and work requires that you stop thinking about seeking a state of perfect equilibrium in your life. It requires you to clearly identify what is important to you and to put yourself at the center of your life. This is how I've seen undeterred women be most successful at integrating life and work. They are not the satellites or the moons on the outskirts of the solar system, but rather the sun in the middle.

Here's how Maisa Batayneh, the first woman in my research to speak about the idea of the second shift, drew a picture to explain her work-life decision-making process to me. In her illustration she attributed different levels of priority and intensity to parts of her life.

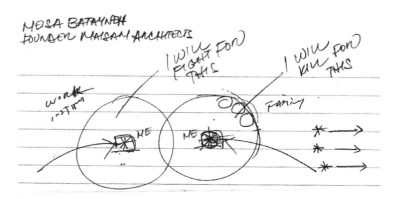

Maisa talked about how she thinks of her life not as "homecentric" or "workcentric," but "me-centric." She thinks about her goals and what she wants to accomplish at work and with her family. She explained that she holds fast to and fights for what she wants and needs at work. On the home front, the stakes are even higher.

On the other side of the world, I had a similar conversation with Flavia De Hora, a managing director at Accenture in Brazil and the firm's most senior woman in the country. I spoke with Flavia in one of Accenture's large, open meeting rooms with huge glass windows and a breathtaking view of Rio de Janeiro. The room was buzzing with several groups of consultants having their own meetings. Flavia had a calming presence. She was soft-spoken and exhibited powerful, yet quiet boldness and authority.

When I asked Flavia about her keys to success, she shared something she thought might be a bit provocative, "In my case, the correct answer is to be a little bit selfish. Women are so worried about what others think, what others say, and what others need. I think what's most important is for me to understand what makes me feel happy, what makes me feel okay and what I like to do every day."

Before you get the wrong impression that Flavia is selfish, let me assure you that she is one of the warmest, most caring people you'd ever want to meet. She is an involved mother, a devoted wife, and at work thinks first about serving her clients and second about mentoring and developing women.

How does Flavia incorporate being a "little bit selfish" into all these roles? Like Maisa, her starting point is herself—what makes her feel best and what she likes to do. Through analysis of what she enjoys most, Flavia figured out the type of client to whom she can provide the most value. She also realized that leading Accenture's women's initiatives, which include formal mentoring and training, energizes her. At home Flavia sends her children off to school with their father and starts her day on the right foot by running along the beach. If you lived in Rio you, too, would want to start your day running on the beach!

On the day of our interview it was Flavia's birthday. She shared that she wanted to celebrate with her husband and friends, but knew her children would also want to spend time with her, so she had arranged to have her mother bring her kids to the restaurant where she would be celebrating to spend a little time with her before their grandmother took them home. She planned to stay to enjoy the rest of the night.

Gordana summed the importance of being at the center of your own life like this: "Don't let them tell you if it is possible to have it all or not. How could somebody possibly know what is 'all' to you? And why are we torturing ourselves with this question anyway? Have you ever seen a male-oriented article with this 'having it or not having it all' bullshit (pardon my language)? Our biggest problem is that from the cradle on, everybody is telling us what is good for us women, what we should do or shouldn't do. Mostly they teach us how to please men and everybody else around us. We are taught how to be good wives to men who are rarely taught how to be good husbands. After you finally allow yourself to be sometimes the sun and not the satellite running around it, your life will start to balance more and more, and it will make you and people around you happier."

WORK-LIFE IMBALANCE

The consequences of not properly blending your work and personal life may be:

- *Lack of fulfillment.* Focusing solely on work (even if you love it) can ultimately lead to a dangerously narrow focus that leaves you feeling depressed when the work is not there.
- *Fatigue.* Depriving yourself of downtime, sleep, breaks, exercise, and recreation will lead to low energy that will then negatively affect your career goals. You will simply burn out.

- *Lost time with family and friends.* Don't promise to spend more time with your spouse or children after you achieve certain career goals. You will always be busy, and there will always be new goals.
- *Poor productivity and performance.* Your work suffers when you have tunnel vision on work and never balance it with leisure activities. If you're able to step away at least occasionally, however, you will refresh your mind and your attitude. Studies show that blending work properly with personal life and outside pursuits results in happier and more successful careers.

WAYS TO CUSTOMIZE YOUR LIFE

An integrated life is something we strive for and sometimes attain. But also be prepared for the times—the hours, days, weeks, months, and perhaps even, but hopefully not, years—when things don't work the way you want them to. You might not be able to take the assignment you need in order to accelerate your professional success. You may have to miss an important time in your child's life. The time you spend with your partner or by yourself may be limited. But in these cases, please understand that this is not a failure. Before you know it, something will shift and you will once again have the peace of mind you seek. Whatever choices you make, don't compare yourself to anyone else, don't presume that anyone's life is easier than yours and don't criticize anyone else's decisions and choices.

One way to think about achieving work-life integration is similar to the way a jazz musician plays music. Jazz musicians improvise around a predetermined progression of chords. A jazz musician interprets a tune in an individual way based on her musical background, heritage, or education, and personal experiences. The way the notes are rearranged and integrated can dramatically change the way a song sounds. So, too, it is with integrating work with your life. Child care, working, and household chores are like chords. The way you choose to improvise around them will be based on your heritage, experiences, values, and what you want your life to be like. Each of us is trying to do the best we can. Here are a few things to keep in mind as you do.

Start with your life goals. Go back to the exercises you did in Chapter 6. Notice if your current work goals and life goals are competing. It's okay if they are, but be realistic about what you will need to do to get both types of goals accomplished. Make sure that integration is the foundation of all your goals so you don't feel that you are accomplishing one at the expense of the other.

Create a schedule that works for you. If you work best with clear division, set specific boundaries for work and personal priorities. If you need more flexibility, don't establish a hard line between work hours and non-work hours, or between work hours and home hours. Know and specifically define what flexibility looks like for you. For some women, work can be done during non-work hours, and flexibility for other life priorities can be provided at work.

Make a decision every day about how you want to focus each part of your day. Consider self, family, work, and community. Create your calendar and schedule it this same way. Prioritize making time for yourself.

Accept that interruptions will inevitably be part of life and work. Don't be frustrated by them. Take the necessary time to address issues and go back to the activity you were engaged in.

Say no to the things that don't fit with your priorities and goals. This presupposes that you know what your goals and priorities are. Refer to your notes from the exercises in Chapter 6. While interruptions from each aspect of your life are inevitable, the only way to achieve your life and work goals is to keep unimportant things from encroaching upon your time. One of my favorite pieces of advice on this topic is "No is a complete sentence."

Make a list of what you will stop doing. Closely related to the last action, make a list of things that you will stop doing in order to make time for the things you want and need to do.

When it doesn't work, try something else. I hope you noted that I said *when*, not *if*, it doesn't work. Remember, your goal is to be undeterred, to find solutions. You want, and deserve, what you want. You are resourceful, you have ideas, and you can ask other women what they do. You can come up with another approach.

When all is said and done, and you have done what you can to design an integrated life, if your work environment still does not accommodate your other life priorities, then you still have one more option: You can vote with your feet and your skills. You can find another job or create one. You are educated, prepared, focused, and undeterred. You are ready for an integrated life!

As you make the right choices for yourself and your family, keep a few things in mind. If you are not working because you have made the decision to be home with your children or because you are unable to find work, you can still use the time to advance your skills in ways that will help you if you decide to return to work and when you find work in the future. To build your skills, consider volunteer activities, participating in networking events, going to conferences, and attending training programs.

If you are not working because you believe your husband or someone else can "take care of you," you may wish to take into account the likelihood that your husband will predecease you or the possibility that you may not be married to your current spouse for your entire life or that the "someone" else may not always be able to provide for you. It's always a good idea to mitigate risks like these by keeping your skills current and your social and professional network alive. Do it just in case you decide or need to take care of yourself.

NO SUCH THING AS A MISSED OPPORTUNITY

I am going to end this chapter with the woman I started it with, Haifa Dia Al-Attia, CEO of the Queen Rania Foundation in Jordan. She says, "Women are often afraid to say no to opportunities at certain points in their careers. You should not worry about missing opportunities. Sometimes you have to make decisions that allow you to be at peace with yourself. I believe that strongly." For Haifa, work-life integration has meant placing her husband and kids prominently in her life while she steadily pursues her career goals. While there may have been times along her career trajectory where she was judged on how her personal life and commitment to her family influenced her career decisions, she always remained true to her priorities, even as she continued to build her expertise and experience. She believed that her achievements would be recognized.

As is fitting for someone who drives education reform and believes that education is the key to long-term prosperity, Haifa's career is steeped in education. She started in a teaching post at the Ministry of Education, worked in the Office of the Crown Prince, and then helped found the Amman Baccalaureate School, where she served for twenty-three years on the board of trustees. She championed equal access to international baccalaureate programs worldwide. In 2006, Haifa joined the Aga Khan Academies as a consultant and helped set up eighteen schools in fourteen developing countries.

While producing results and adding value along the way in each role she undertook, Haifa made many choices. After an injury in 2008 that took eighteen months to heal, she had to slow down. There were times when she dedicated a great deal of time to caring for her mother, and others during which she focused primarily on her children and husband. She spoke about each of these choices as her responsibility and about stepping up to accept them in the same way that she accepted her responsibilities at work. At the same time she continued carefully choosing challenging assignments that developed her knowledge and skills.

Ultimately, Haifa says she is, "Exactly where I want to be. All the work has paid off. I respect myself and the decisions I made. I don't feel that I compromised anything." In 2012, a woman in Haifa's network was asked to recommend someone for the role of CEO of the Queen Rania Foundation. She offered up Haifa's name. Then, her resume and past accomplishments took over. At fifty-nine, Haifa was not surprised to be chosen for the post. Even so, she feels privileged because she knows that she earned it while living her life in her own uncompromised way.

NOW IT'S YOUR TURN

Instead of thinking about if you can "have it all," think about designing your life so you may have what matters to you. Consider your own personal and family needs, as well as your values, career aspirations, and goals. Think also about the support you need and want to receive, especially the emotional support and the money that's required to have the life you envision. Given everything involved in creating an integrated life, how could your wants and needs look like anyone else's? Your life goals are individual to you.

⊘ SELF-REFLECTION: WHAT DOES YOUR CUSTOMIZED LIFE LOOK LIKE?

Start by envisioning what your integrated life looks like and how you'd like each piece of your life (you, your family, work, friends, and other interests) to fit together. If you cannot envision how they integrate, it will be impossible for anyone else (your husband, boss, family, and so on) to do so. Seek your own "right" combination between the amount of time needed for work and at home, between work and family needs, between work and play, and between your own needs and desires and those of others.

Your vision should answer the following questions.

1. What do you want your integrated life to look like?
   Examples: Think about commitments you want to make to family or community; about hours or times you want to commit to work; about a person whose integrated life you respect. How do they do it? Think about what you want realistic days to look like in your integrated life.

2. Next, ask:
   - How much do I want to work?
   - How hard am I willing to work?
   - How much time do I want outside of work?
   - How do I want to spend my time outside work?
   - What level of stress am I willing to have at work and in the rest of my life?
   - How much responsibility do I want to have at work?
   - How much responsibility do I want to have at home?

3. What measures will you use to know when and if you have achieved an integrated life?
   Examples: You are able to get home from work to participate in some of your children's activities. You have time to be alone with your husband. You schedule for yourself and the activities you care about. You are spending sufficient time focused on your job or business to produce stellar results.

These indicators should be directly linked to your definition of success.

ACTIONS
TO CUSTOMIZE YOUR LIFE

At the beginning of this book, I talked about how challenging problems are often best solved by taking a series of repeated actions. This advice is applicable here. You could choose to view the challenge of fitting work into life as intractable; after all, it is arguably an age-old problem, one that some would say has dogged every woman who ever worked outside her home. Or you could do what millions of women around the world do every day, and make work-life integration a habit comprised of many small steps. Stitched together, these create the rich fabric of your life.

Think about your integrated life in four main quadrants:

Self	Family
Work	Community

An integrated life is not a matter of spending equal amounts of time in each quadrant, or of one quadrant taking precedence over another. Instead, it's about paying attention to the parts of each of the quadrants that matter most to you. At various times in your life you'll make decisions about how much time you want or need to spend in each quadrant. Be open to changing how much time you spend in each area as you progress in your goals.

Here are some steps you can take.

1. Map out a schedule that accommodates your life and work priorities.
   Recall Reham Thawabi's or Dora Szwarc Hamaoui's schedules from earlier in the chapter as examples.

2. Have a conversation at home about what you want professionally. Share with your family why you want to work, why it's important to you to work, and your ideas about schedule support, and so on. Be sure you outline the roles you'd like your family members to take on. Frame the conversation as an open discussion, not as a demand, and be open to ideas, alternatives, and suggestions made by your loved ones.
   Example: Vania Neves, who first mentioned the glass balls and rubber balls analogy to me, involves her family in the work decisions that will impact her time at home with them. She talks at length with her husband and son about the opportunities she wants and what it will take for her to get them. As she gets their support and input into what she is doing, they better understand why she is away from home. Although she is already an executive, Vania consistently prepares for

and focuses on her success. As a lifelong learner, she decided to pursue a master's degree. She made sure that her husband was part of this decision and that she had his full support to go back to school. One of the ways he supports her is by driving her to and from university for her classes so that they can enjoy that time together.

3. Have a conversation at work about your professional goals in the context of your life's priorities. Schedule a specific time to meet with your manager and your team (if appropriate). Begin by clearly stating how important work is to you and your commitment to the company and your career. Explain that in order to do the best possible job at work, you also need to be able to manage your other life priorities. Simply and directly ask for what you need. If you are asking for flexibility or work schedule changes, be sure you have think through how your work will be handled. Your message will be best received if you thought through the details ahead of time. Remember, no apologies. Give your manager time to consider your needs and get back to you with his/her agreement or alternatives.

4. Don't ask for help. Instead, ask people to do the part they need to do.

    When women ask their husbands, children, or colleagues and staff at work to help them do something, they retain the idea that the task is their responsibility and the other person is merely "helping" them temporarily. If instead, we politely ask the person to do the task, then it becomes their own. For example, instead of saying, "Would you please help me fold the laundry?" say, "The laundry needs to be folded. Please fold it." Instead of saying, "Would you please help me by running this report or creating this presentation?" say, "The client needs this report, please run it."

5. Don't apologize about work at home, and don't apologize about personal or home needs at work.

In your personal life with your family, your partner, and especially with your children and friends, don't apologize for needing to work. Instead be excited and proud about your professional activities. When you are at work, don't apologize about your personal life; be excited about your family and leisure-time interests. Learn to be comfortable with your right to make personal and professional decisions that work best for you. When you are excited about the things you are doing, others will be excited along with you and will understand why you are at the other place, or why you do what brings you fulfillment. If you talk about work as drudgery and you constantly apologize, those around you will see this and perhaps attempt to make you feel guilty. If you apologize for your needs and the needs of your family, then your coworkers won't be conditioned to understand and respect your priorities. Many of us are conditioned to apologize for anything that affects other people. Stopping this habit can feel foreign, uncomfortable, or even dangerous to our relationships. However, the people around you will start to see that you have not changed your personality or sold out your culture, but that you have simply become more secure in how you operate at work and in your life. Maintain the respectful and courteous habits central to your culture and the need to apologize will fade away.

Although on the surface not apologizing may seem like a minor tactic, it's actually much more significant than that because it has to do with your mindset and how you communicate. It is a very tangible action that you can use to begin to change the conversation about your priorities. You will also begin to see a shift in how your family, those around you, and your employer think about you regarding your work and personal life. Best of all, not being apologetic really works!

COMMUNICATE WITHOUT APOLOGIZING

DON'T SAY ...	INSTEAD SAY ...
At home: "I am so sorry I won't be able to be home for dinner tonight. I have a meeting."	"I have an important meeting tonight that will (explain its relevance or how it helps you with your work). It will be great to catch up and hear about your day when I get home."
At home: "I am so sorry, Mommy can't take you to/pick you up from school tomorrow."	Guess what I get to do tomorrow? I am going to X. What fun things are you going to get to do at school tomorrow? You'll be going to school with Y. It will be fun to catch up on what happened during our day when we see each other later."
At work: "I am so sorry, but I have to leave to pick up my kid (or go to the doctor, go out with my husband, and so on)."	"I've got to head out now to X. I'll work on this tomorrow/later tonight. We'll get it done."

Look how far you have come. You've been preparing for your success and focusing on what's most important to you. Now you have envisioned and planned for the integrated life you want. The next step is to figure out how to accelerate the success you've defined.

SUMMARY

To develop your integrated mindset, stop viewing life and work as either one or the other, combine them. Define what a successful integrated life looks like for you, and know that it will be different from most other women's lifestyles. Look at your life and your priorities. Use the focus habit to define your success. Then determine how the people around you can help you create the life you desire, and leverage the resources you need. Finally, make specific and careful schedules so that your work and life fit well together.

Choosing to build an integrated life may require adjusting many things at home and at work, but it will be one of the best decisions you can make for your happiness and personal definition of success.

NOTES

GO

— HABIT 5 —

Accelerate

"What got you here won't get you there."
Marshall Goldsmith
Executive and leadership coach

IN OVER TWENTY YEARS GUIDING WOMEN IN THEIR careers, I've encountered far too many situations like the following. My client, a highly qualified woman, had worked for her employers for over ten years. Based on her performance, she had earned expanded roles. Then she got stuck. She had ambitions well beyond her current role and her company also saw a lot of future potential in her. No matter how hard she worked, however, the next opportunity she was yearning for didn't come along.

When I started coaching her, I observed her interactions in the workplace, asked questions, and got to know as much as I could about the way she worked. I determined that my client's career stall could not be attributed to the part of the business she worked in, which is sometimes an issue for women if they're working in the less-valued parts of their organizations. It also wasn't due to a lack of results or poor interpersonal skills. Rather, her progress was inhibited by other behaviors she was demonstrating. It was evident to me that:

- Although she was a strategic thinker—a critically important and highly valued skill required to reach a senior leadership role—my client rarely shared her strategic insights.

- She regularly shared with teammates how hard she was working, how late she was working, how much she was working, and how tired she was. At times, she looked a bit frazzled. She neglected to share, however, that she relished and thrived on hard work.

- Her high level of intelligence enabled her to maneuver the difficult problems encountered in her area of expertise better than anyone who worked for her. As a result, she often did not delegate.

- My client worked so hard that she didn't make time to network either inside or outside the company. As a result, not many people knew her.

Early in her career my client had been told to keep her head down, do good work, and produce results. Those behaviors had worked for her up to this point. Why weren't they working anymore? The answer, coined and widely spread by renowned executive coach Marshall Goldsmith, was: "What got you here won't get you there."[1] My client needed a different approach in order to advance further in her career. Once she understood this, she started putting the new strategies into place.

Her seemingly intractable, systemic problem was ultimately solved by repeatedly performing a few key actions, the kind I've discussed throughout this book. She:

- Learned to share her strategic perspective in every meeting. She had previously felt uncomfortable with the male-dominated style of communication, where the men spoke over each other and interrupted frequently, so she had actually been raising her hand, like a schoolgirl, to speak! She stopped doing that and learned how to jump in.

- Offered her views, even if her thoughts were not entirely defined. In the past, she'd waited to completely formulate ideas before speaking. She learned that no one expected her to have fully formed ideas. It was okay if her ideas were not fully thought through and did not get traction—even if they were shot down. She recognized that waiting until she had everything "figured out" was in some ways selfish and mistrusting of her teammates. If she believed in her team and in their abilities to contribute, then she could throw out an idea and be confident that they could shape it better together than she could on her own.

- Stopped talking so much about her workload and how tired she was. These stories had made executive management afraid to give her more responsibility, for fear she could not manage it successfully.

- Identified the work that *only* she could do and began to delegate the rest. Delegating freed her to think more strategically (her strength) and to begin to expand and deepen her network.

- Identified key people inside the company where she worked, as well people in her industry at large, that she would regularly connect by phone or email, and in person. Then, in internal meetings, she shared what she had learned from her network.

- Identified and participated in a rigorous and very prestigious professional development program that leveraged her innovative skills.

- Took on visible, challenging assignments that were of critical value to the interests of the company.

- Ensured that her valuable accomplishments were visible to management.

- Made her desires for a broader opportunity known.

It didn't take long. A few months after my client put these acceleration tactics into practice, she was recognized for contributing more broadly—and she was promoted!

WAYS TO ACCELERATE SUCCESS

If you are just graduating from college or early in your career, I want you to know something very important. The approach that has made you successful up to this point is only part of the approach that will make you successful in your career or business. Girls usually learn early on to work hard, to "be good," and not to be too loud or boisterous, to do their work and not be too disruptive. These are all good attributes and they may have served you well. But to make career progress or succeed as a businesswoman, you need different skills: working smart, not hard; speaking up, not being quiet; disrupting the workplace with your ideas; not keeping your head down, but keeping your head up; feeling strong about yourself and meeting others eye to eye. In fact, make a point to look around and connect with people everywhere you go.

Acceleration is the most tangible and straightforward of all the undeterred success habits. It involves implementing a set of specific and well-defined, time-tested actions. These actions will take you where you want to go more quickly and easily. Some of these are personal actions. Others require support. To accelerate your success:

- Take on high-profile assignments and business opportunities.
- Deliver results.
- Strengthen your support network.
- Make your achievements known.
- Ask for what you want.

In the next two chapters, I'm going to give you the strategies that will help you become more notable and ways to strengthen your business network. Use these strategies to proactively manage your career and business success.

Having read this far and done the exercises in Parts One and Two, you are ready to take off! You are emotionally and professionally prepared. You're focused. You know your definition of success, and you've set goals to realize your vision. You've figured out how to blend your work into your life. Your next steps are to make notable contributions and to get the support you need to accelerate your success.

NOTES

BE NOTABLE, MAKE AN IMPACT

CHAPTER 8

CONTRIBUTE

*Make your achievements
notable and known.*

THE BEST WAYS FOR WOMEN TO ACCELERATE their career advancement are to contribute and make their achievements known. For you to advance, it is imperative that your colleagues, employers, and customers are familiar with the contributions you make and the results you achieve.

A frequently cited study, "The Myth of the Ideal Worker: Does Doing All the Right Things Really Get Women Ahead?" conducted by Catalyst, a research-based organization that promotes inclusive workplaces for women, reveals: "When women were most proactive in making their achievements

> visible they advanced further, were more satisfied with their careers, and had greater compensation growth than women who were less focused on calling attention to their successes. Of all the strategies used by women, making their achievements known—by ensuring their manager was aware of their accomplishments, seeking feedback and credit as appropriate, and asking for a promotion when they felt it was deserved—was the *only one* associated with compensation growth."[1]

Unfortunately, self-promotion is often one of the hardest success behaviors for women in growth economies to adopt. You may be nodding your head in agreement, and perhaps you can personally identify with the reluctance that some women have to seek attention and promote themselves. Particularly in regions of the Middle East, Asia, and Africa, women are taught not to call attention to themselves; to listen, not talk; and to stay out of the spotlight. But for you to get ahead in your business or career, people must know who you are and why they should work with you. So, you have to find ways that are comfortable for you to share your knowledge, accomplishments, and capabilities. You must be notable.

Even if a businesswoman is from a country or culture where people typically do not call attention to themselves and women are expected to be modest, quiet, and humble, there are ways she can make herself visible. Although I'm not talking just about making yourself physically visible, here's the very memorable way by which Saudi Arabian business leader Dr. Manar Al-Moneef made herself notable.

Dr. Al-Moneef was invited to speak at an event in her country where she was told that she would have to give her presentation from behind a screen so that she would not be visible to the male conference attendees. As you may be aware, social custom in Saudi Arabia often dictates that men and women be physically separated in public. She refused.

Hearing Dr. Al-Moneef's refusal, the conference organizers were distraught and didn't know what to do. But she told them not to worry; she had a solution. She had no desire to offend, but she also didn't want to lose a valuable opportunity for her message to be clearly heard—and for that, the entire audience would need to both hear and *see her*.

Prior to coming on the stage, she called out to the audience from behind the curtain, saying, "Anyone who does not wish to see me, I'll give you a few minutes before I come out to turn your chair around to face the back of the room." Nobody did!

WAYS TO BE NOTABLE

One of the most important and distinguishing actions of women who accelerate their careers is that they make themselves visible. They achieve tangible business results, communicate their achievements, seize opportunities, ask for what they want, and convey professional presence.

Achieve tangible business results. The importance of delivering business results is a topic often shortchanged in the professional advice given to women. In their efforts to empower women, many advisors forget that success, at its core, first and foremost depends on making a contribution. In order to have the ability to make a significant contribution, you will need to have expertise. Gain expertise by continually developing deep, up-to-date business and field-specific knowledge and skills—not just interpersonal and leadership skills. Undeterred women adopt a habit of lifelong learning to build the expertise they need to deliver results.

While how you do your job is extremely important, accelerating your success hinges on whether or not you actually create tangible business outcomes. Delivering results means that you accomplish your tasks and then go beyond what you were asked to do in order to make real business contributions to your organization. Undeterred women produce bottom-line results that add value to their companies and their clients.

Dr. Al-Moneef had an opportunity for career growth when she was offered a job at the Saudi Arabian General Investment Authority (SAGIA). She knew that if she were going to make the transition from a practicing physician to a business leader, she would need to develop her business skills. She applied for and received a scholarship from Harvard Business School in the United States for an executive education program. Her expanded expertise enabled her to provide strategic and technical input and build strategy-driven revenue business models for SAGIA.

Because of her contributions she was offered the position of Director General of Health Care and Life Sciences at SAGIA.

As I explained in Chapter 4, the best way to develop your skills is through on-the-job experience, rather than from professional training programs. Many women fail to advance in their careers or businesses because they have not had the experiences required for continued advancement. These include essential experiences such as working in the core revenue-generating functions of a company, having responsibility for creating profits and managing expenses, and taking on high-profile, high-risk, and challenging assignments. Understanding this, Chinese journalist Zhen Wang asked for the work experience that would further develop her skills so she could contribute to the core business of her employer. Because of her already great English skills, Hu Shuli, the then-chief editor of *Caijing Magazine* where Zhen worked, wanted Zhen to work as the publication's English editor and translator. But Zhen knew that to develop and get ahead she needed to work in the core business of a news journal: in news production.

Zhen explained what she did. "After working 50 percent of the time as an English editor and 50 percent as a Chinese reporter, I told Ms. Hu that I wanted to be a 100 percent Chinese reporter and not be given anymore translation assignments. This was a hard choice because people think that my English skills bring more value to the news journal than my work as a journalist. Speaking for myself, I believe I can make the best use of my English language by interviewing a lot of English-speaking people."

Communicate your achievements. Undeterred women deliver results and make their achievements known to influential people. They know that their results won't speak for themselves. They know that what speaks loudest for a job well done is when they and their supporters make their achievements known.

Chinese journalist Jennifer Cheung explained how she landed a full-time editorial position at China Labour Bulletin (CLB), a non-profit that advocates labor rights for Chinese workers. "CLB hired me because I used to blog extensively on China's human rights issues and had a network of Chinese Internet activists."

Seize opportunities. Denise Abulafia, Ph.D., an Argentinian scientist, researcher, and university professor, had an idea for a company. At a birthday party for one of her kid's friends, she met Nicolas Berman, a top mentor for the owners of startups and mentioned her business idea to him in passing. Nicolas invited Denise to follow up with a meeting at his office so he could hear more about her idea. While they were still at the party, she emailed him to set up the appointment.

How often are any of us given opportunities that we fail to follow up on? Not Denise. She was ready and jumped at the opportunity presented to her. She wasn't afraid Nicolas might say no to her—and she wasn't afraid he might say yes. She did not shy away from asking for what she wanted because she didn't want to appear "too ambitious" or "greedy," or because she was afraid that if she did voice her needs and they were not met she might feel that she had failed or that others would know she was not successful. She just went for it.

Denise understood how important it was to communicate her accomplishments and abilities, as well as her vision for her future business. She knew that would be how she'd get support for her business idea. Because of her ideas, insights, and experience, people such as Nicolas Berman were willing to meet with her.

Ask for what you want. There are countless studies that indicate that women don't ask for what they want and there are many others that refute those findings. These studies indicate that women do ask, but ask in the wrong ways. As a result, they are not heard or given what they want. One of the best ways to approach getting what you want is to ask for it directly.

Jennifer Cheung shared with me her sense that what has led to her success today is the ability to "identify opportunities and be brave enough to ask." When she was in a media program at the University of Hong Kong, she was eager to get as many experiences as possible to pursue her dream of being a journalist. She took on many news writing assignments in order to secure good internship recommendations. She was successful in getting internships at Voice of America Beijing and *Forbes* magazine.

Jennifer reported, "After my *Forbes* internship, I asked my supervisor if I could be promoted to analyst, a position that would enable me to write in-depth analytic pieces. My supervisor said yes." In the meantime, Jennifer noticed the contributor initiative at Forbes and called her former *Forbes* editor to tell him about her new assignment. He asked her if she would also contribute to *Forbes* on Chinese labor issues, which had become her area of expertise.

In my experience, not all women take opportunities to ask for what they want. Some are skilled at asking, others are not. Only you can determine whether you do or don't ask, and how effective you are in asking for what you want.

Asking for what you want is a straightforward process, but not necessarily an easy one. First, you have to determine the result you want and then figure out how you can make it happen. The challenging part is that you have to communicate what you want with someone who has the authority to make it happen. Prepare for these types of conversations by gathering all the information you need to support your position, and practice what you are going to say ahead of time.

Let me caution you not to inadvertently or unconsciously negotiate against yourself. I see people do that all the time and have caught myself making the same mistake. Recently, I submitted a proposal to a global company for a speaking engagement and some training for a group of high-potential women. The clients called to say they were very pleased with my proposal and wanted to hire me to do the work. As we talked through the proposal, my contact never mentioned the cost, nonetheless I heard myself offering to include more services under the same contract for no additional cost. There was absolutely no reason for me to have done that; I did so because I was feeling insecure and wanted to ensure they hired me. Pay attention to the self-doubt and insecurities that pop up for you and erode the confidence you have been building.

Convey a strong professional presence. To advance, you must exhibit professionalism in the way you speak, how you behave, and how you look. The term most commonly used to describe a person's *presence* in terms of their ability to advance in the workplace is *executive presence.* An authority on this topic is Sylvia Hewlett, who wrote an entire book on the topic titled *Executive Presence: The Missing Link Between Merit and Success.*

I purposefully chose to use the term *professional presence* rather than *executive presence.* While I am essentially referring to the same thing, I know that not everyone wants to become an executive. I did not want you to discount what you read or hear on this topic, thinking that it does not apply to you. In reality your professional presence, regardless of your role, is a key criterion in determining whether you attain positions at many organizational levels of a company or accomplishing your professional goals as an entrepreneur.

Professional presence, especially as it relates to women, is another topic often neglected in the workplace or business community, yet it is a critical part of the success equation.

During the time I was involved in talent planning and executive development at Bank of America, as well as in my subsequent work as a consultant and coach to numerous organizations, I saw many individuals being overlooked for assignments and opportunities because they did not possess all three attributes that are required for success: expertise, results, and professional presence.

Several companies have hired me to coach women (and men) on their professional presence. In some cases, the women I coached spoke too much, repeating themselves over and over without contributing anything new, or gave so much detail that their colleagues were lost in the conversation and could not share their own views. In other instances, my clients did not speak up enough. Even though they had significant insights to offer, they lacked the confidence to share their opinions or knowledge openly.

A third type of communication problem came from clients who did not use the language of business in speaking. In these cases, the women had to adopt a business vocabulary when communicating at work.

Here's how Crystal Yi Wang described the steps she has taken to develop her business acumen. "I work extremely hard during and even after work. I read all kinds of business articles and magazines to pick up the hot topics in commercial areas. I improved my business analytical capability by working long hours every day and spending my personal time reading and thinking.

"Working ten to twelve hours a day is common in a professional services firm. You have to be physically and mentally ready. Sometimes you may need to study a lot of material to understand a new industry in less than a week. You need to spend a lot of time researching, reading, talking to industry experts, brainstorming, and digesting all kinds of information before you even start to work on your deliverables. During our projects, we talk to different kinds of people. The research we do is not as glamorous as people might imagine. If the assignment is a project about the agricultural industry, then we need go to the village and talk to the farmers. To be successful at this job you need to be an open person who enjoys talking to diverse people under different kinds of circumstances. Language capability is also very important. You need to understand, digest, and then use the most precise language to write the key messages you want to deliver. Sometimes, communicating with company owners isn't pleasant.

"I have faced some Chinese company owners who despised me or even doubted my capability because I was a woman and young. As a young woman, you need to do a lot of preparation to equip yourself, and dress as if you are older than you actually are. You are in a disadvantaged position in China's business environment if you are a woman, and you are in an even more disadvantaged position if you are a young woman."

I've also coached women whose appearance was disheveled. Their appearance gave the impression that they were not organized, and at worst, perhaps not competent. In such cases, improving the women's professional presence was a matter of giving them direct, specific feedback so they understood how they were perceived. Then, they had the option to change or else accept the consequences of the impression they made.

I coached a senior-level woman whose conservative company saw potential in her and wanted to promote her to an executive role, but her communication style and appearance did not match the culture of the company where she worked. My client talked way too much and rambled on when the executive team at her firm, which consisted mostly of engineers and financial people, spoke sparingly. My client didn't have much interest in her appearance and often even looked sloppy. Everyone else in the senior team maintained a very sharp polished look.

When my client was first given the feedback that these two areas of her presence were holding back her ascent in the company, she was angry. She knew she had the skills and knowledge to operate at an executive level and didn't understand why she had to talk and look like everyone else. When I first met with her, she also voiced the opinion that this feedback might be a bias against her as a woman. As we explored her organization further, we determined that the feedback she received was similar to that being given to others, and that executive management's expectations of her were the same as those it had for the rest of the executive team (who, not surprisingly, were all male).

Is it right for an organization to want their management teams to look and communicate in a specific way? Are they not valuing diversity by having these expectations? Perhaps. Should they be more open? Most certainly. At that moment, however, it did not change the situation for my client. So I asked her if she aspired to an executive role at her company. When she confirmed that she did and told me again how much she enjoyed where she worked and how fulfilled she was by her job, I told her that she (and all of us) have choices. If she wanted a promotion at the company where she worked, she would need to improve her professional presence. If she didn't want to do that, it was certainly her choice. However, if she chose not to, she likely would be limiting her role at that particular company.

I shared one more thing with my client, something I regularly tell the women I coach and mentor. "If you think the system or the expectations are wrong, one of the best ways, and sometimes the only way, to change it is to get in a decision-making role. It's much easier to change the rules if you are sitting at the decision-making table or have your own table—your own business. If you think the expectations you face are completely inappropriate, then take action by speaking with someone who has the power and influence to make a change or by leaving the company."

Some people incorrectly assume that professional presence is all about appearance, so they focus much of their attention on how they dress, when in fact, the outfits you wear are only one aspect of presence. Other people neglect their appearance entirely and look unprofessional, or their style seems out of place among their colleagues. As a businesswoman, remember that your appearance counts. You can have your own unique style, but this style must fit within cultural, company-wide, and industry norms. Your goal is to be identified by what you contribute, not by what you wear.

I have seen many women elevate their professional presence. One striking example is Brazilian Renata Pessoa. I first met Renata when she was participating in the highly selective International Women's Forum Fellows Program, a year-long program designed to develop the leadership and strategic capabilities of high-potential women from all over the world. Renata's results in managing significant client relationships had gotten her into the very competitive program, but when I met her it was evident that she would need to develop in additional ways to get further ahead at Accenture. Renata was clearly smart and accomplished, but she was also rather shy and unassuming.

Renata and I kept in touch. When I met Renata again, in Rio de Janeiro in November 2013, she had been promoted to the position of managing director. I could immediately see a change in her. She was more confident. The way she carried herself, dressed, and the way she spoke was different. The woman I met this time was self-assured. She stood straighter and her entire appearance was more polished. She spoke succinctly, in business terms and without hesitation about her current role and her approach to achieve challenging business objectives with which she had been tasked. As a result of her transformation and the new measure of confidence she felt, Renata had offered several impressive strategic ideas to her client and to Accenture.

NOW IT'S YOUR TURN

To accelerate your career success, contribute results, make your achievements known, and cultivate a strong professional presence.

SELF-REFLECTION: IDENTIFY OPPORTUNITIES TO CONTRIBUTE

Answer the following three questions to determine where you can best contribute.

- How does my company or business succeed in the marketplace? What financial, strategic, and customer measures are most important for its success?
  Examples: Through customer acquisition, large contracts, or new product launches.

- Where and how do I fit into the essential, most valued parts of the business? Which of my skills and competencies could make the best contribution?
  Examples: Social media, contract negotiation, financial analysis, or strategic product innovation.

- Which of these competencies do I most enjoy? And which comes most easily to me?

 ## ACTIONS
TO CONTRIBUTE RESULTS

Here are some of the specific actions I share when I coach my clients to accelerate their success. Once you have determined the metrics and levers that drive performance where you work, find ways to deliver results in those areas. The best way to do that is to:

- Identify one or two areas of opportunity for your company or industry that intersect with your interests, strengths, and areas of expertise.

- Determine a specific outcome you can achieve in this area/these areas.

- Make time in your schedule to work on the area or areas you identify.

→ ACTIONS TO COMMUNICATE YOUR CONTRIBUTIONS

Take the following steps to communicate your contributions.

1. For every one of your significant accomplishments, identify specifically whom you should share the achievement with.
   Examples: My manager, an influential leader, or my mentor.

2. Determine the most strategic timing for you to communicate. Assess when your communication will be

best received and won't get buried under a mountain of other information.

3. Determine how you will make your accomplishment known to your manager and influential others. *Examples: Send a note or email. Verbally share your achievement. Find someone who is willing to share news of your achievement on your behalf. Take out an advertisement in a trade publication. Write an article.*

4. Share the outcomes you produce, not just activities you are engaged in. Describe your contributions in a manner consistent with the way that people in your industry, community, or company measure results. Use business language and measures of performance that are understood and valued in your field.

5. For really notable achievements, consider applying for, or being nominated for an award or competition.

   There are numerous recognition initiatives for businesswomen all over the world. There may even be some at your place of employment. Do some research online to identify programs and ask your mentors, network, or businesswomen's organization about such programs they may know of. These recognition programs are an excellent way for you to indirectly communicate news of your achievements and become better known in the business community.

Select one or more of these approaches, or identify another way that feels comfortable and is appropriate in your culture. You don't have to brag, and your communication style can be humble, but you must find a way to make your successes known.

 ## ACTIONS
TO ACKNOWLEDGE YOUR CONTRIBUTIONS

My mother always told me that when someone pays you a compliment, it is exactly the same as if they had given you a gift. The appropriate response when someone gives you a gift is to say, "Thank you." So why, when most of us have been taught to be kind and gracious, can we not accept compliments or positive feedback?

Every time your performance or results are recognized, thank the person recognizing you, then accept and take credit for the result rather than dismissing, diminishing, or minimizing your performance. Because acknowledging and communicating your contributions is so important to raising your visibility and accelerating your success, following are some specific ways you can do so.

INSTEAD OF SAYING THINGS LIKE . . .	SAY . . .
When someone acknowledges one of your accomplishments: • "We have been given many opportunities." • "I have a great team." • "We've been lucky."	• "Thank you. I have I am proud/pleased with my role (leading or as a member of our team) and the results achieved." • "Thank you. I worked hard (along with the team) to make this successful." • "Thank you. I am glad that you see my hard work (and my team's work) reflected in our results."
When someone compliments one of your ideas: "It was nothing, everyone has good ideas."	"Thank you. I'm glad my input was helpful and can add value to our work."
When someone presents you with an opportunity: "I hope I can meet your expectations."	"Thank you. I look forward to making a significant contribution."

ACTIONS
TO BUILD YOUR PROFESSIONAL PRESENCE

Your professional presence also sends messages about your goals to those around you. As you think about strengthening your presence, take the following actions.

- Speak like a businessperson.
  Examples: Communicate in a direct, crisp, and succinct way. Have an expert grasp of the business terminology and vocabulary of your field. Use this language as your means to contribute your best business insights or ideas.

- Maintain an appearance that's in line with company-wide, industry, and cultural norms even as it expresses your personal style. Avoid dishevelment.

- Behave in a manner that is consistent with cultural and corporate norms.

- Be poised.
  Examples: Project confidence. Demonstrate calm and control. Emulate the most successful people around you. Communicate clearly and maintain your composure.

To maintain composure under any circumstances, pay attention to the overall impression you make. Everything matters, including how you stand, sit, look, talk, and react.

If conforming to cultural or business expectations creates too much tension for you and requires you not to be true to yourself, then adapting is not right for you. Just be aware that the world probably won't mold itself to your preferences. If you want to develop your professional presence, try these specific communication techniques.

IF YOU HAVE A TENDENCY TO ...	INSTEAD ...
Talk too much	• **Start in the middle.** When you want to communicate something, don't start at the beginning of the story or incident, start from the middle. Remember, people will ask if they need more background information. • **Pick**. If you have five things you want to say, pick the most important three. If you have three things you want to say, pick two. • **Visualize a traffic sign**. When you start talking, visualize that the light is green for one minute. After one minute, the light turns orange. At that point you have thirty seconds to find a clear indication that your audience is engaged and actively listening to you. If they are, you may talk for another minute before the light turns red. If not, slow down at orange and ask if they want you to continue or have any questions.

Speak too little	• **Look for a pause** in conversation when others are talking, and insert your perspective. • **Tell a trusted coworker or your manager** that you are working on communicating more frequently. Ask your ally to bring you into more conversations by asking you questions or referencing your areas of expertise.
Speak primarily in tactical terms	• **Prepare** a strategic point of view before every meeting or important conversation. • **Group** your comments under strategic statements or categories.
Speak too casually and not use business terms	• **Listen** to those around you who use business terminology well. Notice which business terms and metrics they use, and follow their example. • **Learn** how your company makes money and what it values by speaking with your manager, a financial person, or by reading. Incorporate financial metrics and things that are important to your company, business, or industry when you talk about your own work.

Get flustered	• **Anticipate** negative triggers and prepare in advance how you will deal with them. • **Take a deep breath** and silently, slowly count to ten before you speak. • **Stand firmly.** Sometimes something as seemingly small as how you stand can affect the way you respond. Observe your standing or sitting posture, and adjust it accordingly so that you feel firmly anchored when you deliver your message.

SUMMARY

To accelerate your success, keep growing and learning. Acquire and continue to develop the interpersonal, managerial, leadership, and technical skills required to excel in your field.

You will need to seek new skill-development opportunities even if you are content in your current position or business. Otherwise you will start to decline, sometimes even unconsciously. Professionally speaking, staying still results in decline. No one ever overcame a barrier or obstacle by standing still.

You have to fly above, not below the radar. By that, I mean that you and your results must be visible and notable. The ways to become notable are to:

- Achieve tangible business results.
- Communicate your achievements.
- Convey a strong professional presence.

NOTES

NURTURE
YOUR
NETWORK

CHAPTER 9

CONNECT

"The more you give, the more you get."
Lyubov Simonova
Russian venture capitalist

In addition to actions you personally take to accelerate your success, you will need support from others around you to take full advantage of opportunities. A strong base of support includes a robust business network, mentors, and a sponsor.

BUILD AND NURTURE A NETWORK

Successful women have a diverse network of role models and people they count on, and who count on them. These networks help you with information, introductions, business, and support. The purpose of networking is for you and the people in your network to mutually generate career and business opportunities.

Connections, referrals, and networks are critical to conducting business. In China, the term *guanxi* is used to refer to the intricate network of contacts that a person can rely on when something needs to be done. Russian venture capitalist Lyubov Simonova framed the importance of strong connections in this way. "I encourage women never to forget that life is given only once, so you need to make it full of great moments for yourself and everybody around you. The more you give, the more you get. This rule works the same in the field of business as the field of life."

Networks are important for two primary reasons. First, personal relationships help you achieve work results. Second, if you network with the right group of diverse people, you will gather market, industry, and company information you could not get from any other source.

Building a network does not mean just going to networking events, getting your LinkedIn profile updated, and getting lots of connections on online social networks, although it does include these elements. The most important thing to know before you network is the reason why you are reaching out to connect with someone. Having a clear purpose will greatly improve your connection and increase the potential of getting what you want.

This goes back to having focus. Aimlessly meeting people without knowing why is socializing, not networking. It can take up a lot of your time and not result in the type of support you need or want to give.

Think of building your professional network on all of the following levels. Regularly connect:

Up. With your manager and more senior or influential people in your industry or field.

Down. With your staff or junior people where you work or within your community.

In. Within your organization or industry, and especially with peers.

Out. With knowledgeable people outside your company, especially well-connected women and men.

WAYS TO NETWORK

There are many different ways to network and many books and articles written on the topic. As you develop your support base, I encourage you to seek out additional resources to guide you. Earlier in this book, I outlined a few widely known ways to build support including joining business-affiliated networks and attending events. Here are a few more examples of how undeterred women build and maintain their networks.

Participate in a business accelerator or incubator. Both business accelerators and incubators prepare companies for growth. Business acceleration programs usually last three to six months. The time an entrepreneur spends in an incubator is typically much longer, sometimes years, and often includes various forms of mentorship and support.

When a friend told Croatian entrepreneur Ana Kolarević, about a local startup incubator in Zagreb, she applied for and attended one of their events. "In the beginning, I was scared because I didn't know anyone at the first event, and didn't know what to expect," Ana said. "It seemed closed off. But I just started shaking hands and talking to people. After that the first event, I knew people at the second event, and so on." Ana credits the startup community in Zagreb for being a key part of her ability to succeed each step of the way. It has become her strong support network.

Connect with people one on one. Algerian Leila Rezaiguia, calls herself an "extreme extrovert and networker by nature." Leila enjoys connecting people who she thinks have something in common or might be able to help one another. One of the first places Leila starts is LinkedIn.com, a business-oriented online social network used primarily for professional networking. Her personal profile there is well established and highlights her skills, talents, and past work experience. Whenever she meets someone in person, she invites that individual to join her LinkedIn community. She spends time each week reaching out to her individual connections on LinkedIn to ask them to meet her for a cup of coffee one on one.

Leila asserts, "Keeping my network alive is perhaps the biggest thing that has gotten me where I am in my career. For example, a past client from an old job is currently my business partner and cofounder. Because I stayed in touch with him, we became friends, and this allowed us to start our business together last year."

If networking is difficult or intimidating for you, Leila has a good piece of advice to keep in mind. "It comes down to knowing what you have in common with the person you are talking to. What is it that makes this person tick? How are you connected? Maybe it is your language, being from the same country, food you both like, sports, a passion, or so on. We can find something in common with almost everyone. I maintain relationships with the people whom I click with. I make sure to reach out to them every now and again and ask to meet for lunch, dinner, or coffee. Or I invite them to a seminar they might like."

Participate in online networks. Networking is not only about going to lots of events, although it often takes that form. Some women fear networking. They feel shy and uncomfortable at large events or when faced with the prospect of approaching people they don't know. They may have had tough experiences attending an event where they didn't know anyone, didn't feel included or welcomed, and had a hard time breaking into circles of people who already seemed connected. (I've had that experience myself many times in my career.)

If you are uncomfortable in group situations, choose the events you attend carefully. Focus your efforts instead on one-on-one networking opportunities, and on keeping in touch electronically and through social media such as online communities, chat rooms, as well as emails. Network with people you feel enriched and supported by, people who share your interests, and people you feel good about being with.

In Russia, as it is for people all over the world, establishing a business as a new entrepreneur without a network is quite difficult. Because headhunter Alena Vladimirskaya, the founder and CEO of the recruiting company PRUFFI, had made and nurtured her connections, when she left her corporate job in headhunting to launch her own business, she didn't have this problem. She was already respected and trusted, and clients were eager to work with her. Alena regularly focuses on expanding her network in her own city, country, and even abroad. Her networking is not just about self-promotion, she is also eager to help others along the way. During the past three decades, she has built her expertise, skills, and reputation. Alena observed, "I've learned that in order to be successful, you don't need to be very experienced, you just have to use your resources and your connections smarter." One of the ways in which Alena has built her personal and professional network is through participating in online social networks. She is very active on VK.com, the largest Russian social network in Europe, and on Facebook.

Be a superconnector. As you may imagine, many of the women I met with while conducting the research for this book have strong networks. A few of these women are what I would call superconnectors, women whose networks are made up of many different types of people and whose connections are so strong and so deep that their contacts respond almost immediately to their outreach or requests. In over four years of research, four women stood out as superconnectors: Esmat El Nahas in Egypt, Nabila Marcos in Jordan, Sandra Portugal in Brazil, and Lorena Diaz in Argentina.

Argentinian Lorena Diaz impressed me with the strength of her connections. Lorena is now a consultant, but she was formerly the public relations manager for MercadoLibre, the regional ecommerce platform and principal online auction site for the Spanish- and Portuguese-speaking communities in Latin America. Because Lorena is such an effective networker, I thought you could benefit from her top three tips for building a deep, far-reaching network.

- *Tip 1: Give value and time to others.* Have one-on-one meetings, make Skype calls, go to events, and talk to people through social media. Whenever and however you meet with others, always add value to their needs, activities, hobbies, and so on. For example, refer them to great resources. Of course, in order to do that, you must hear their needs. Pay attention when people talk about what they love doing or need to do. Lorena said, "I send the people I meet interesting links or information every now and then, give them some books, or connect them to other people. I make special space in my agenda once per week to 'give consultancy for free.' I also invest time in teaching. Students can develop interesting careers and are the future door to new, exciting, and younger networks."

- *Tip 2: Be part of different organizations.* Join non-governmental organizations, including chambers of commerce, for example. Not just any NGO or chamber, but those where you are committed to their main topic or mission. Then offer value, your time, and your knowledge.

- *Tip 3: Keep in touch.* When you finish a project or a program such as your MBA, or language classes, or change jobs, put a note in your calendar to call or get in touch on a regular basis with former classmates and colleagues.

Lorena said, "I learned these different best practices in networking from almost all the bosses I've had in my career. I paid a lot of attention to how they built and created their networks. One of them even registered the color preferences of the people in her network in order to customize the presents she gave them. Now that I am a consultant, potential clients call me because they know and trust me. Sometimes they ask about topics or businesses far from my core business. But they know I will do my best to get the answers or find the connections in every situation. Through my involvement in Vital Voices, an NGO that identifies, trains, and empowers emerging women leaders and social entrepreneurs around the globe, I've met people around the world. I have cultivated those relationships and now if I need something from Russia, El Salvador, Washington, Nigeria, or even Kyrgyzstan I know whom to call. This kind of networking clearly requires having a long-term vision and making a big time investment. But you will get much more out of it than you might expect."

COMMON NETWORKING MISTAKES

The most common mistakes I see people make in networking are:

- *Not making enough time to network:* either not networking at all or networking too infrequently.
- *Not having a comprehensive Up, Down, In, and Out networking strategy:* connecting with people who don't broaden their business impact or knowledge base.
- *Only reaching out to people when they need something:* versus developing an ongoing and mutually beneficial relationship.
- *Going to events and talking only to people they already know:* essentially swimming in safe waters instead of broadening and deepening their pool of connections.
- *Networking only with people within their own organization:* not developing a broader external view or contacts in the business community at large.
- *Networking only with people outside their companies:* neglecting the people in their firms and thus not having strong internal alliances. By doing so, they run the risk of being viewed as only interested in their own success versus being seen as collaborative members of their organizations.

- *Not having a networking plan that includes:*
  - Their reason for networking.
  - Networking plan and goals.
  - Identifying key people with whom to build relationships.
  - Identifying the best way to connect with key people with whom they want to establish relationships.
  - Information and insights they can offer and want to receive.
- *Not clearly articulating their career or business goals, aspirations, and what they are working on.* It's not boasting or overly ambitious to be clear about your goals and work. It is only by sharing goals that people can uncover areas of mutual interest and collaboration.
- *Monopolizing networking conversations.* Talking entirely about themselves without thinking about the people they are talking to. A good networker listens, asks questions, and is genuinely interested in the goals and needs of the people they are talking to—not just their own.

DEALING WITH GENDER-RELATED NETWORKING CONSTRAINTS

Cultural norms around acceptable behavior for women in growth economies may make it challenging for you to build and nurture your network. Women around the world regularly bring up the difficulties they face in meeting people with whom they know they should network. I understand and acknowledge these constraints. In some places, like in the Middle East, it is common for businessmen to gather at night in hotels or in someone's home, places where it might not be appropriate for women to be seen, to talk about business. In countries like Russia and China, networking often occurs over drinks late at night, making it difficult for women with children and other responsibilities to participate. Interestingly, these norms now also affect how women network. ReD Associates, an innovation and strategy consulting business, conducted a cross-cultural, ethnographic study of leading global alcohol and beverage brands. The study specifically focused on how women go out and how they consume alcohol. As part of the study, the researchers spent time studying a group of women in emerging economies, among them Lagos, Moscow, Bangkok, Shanghai, Seoul, and Sao Paulo. The study revealed that women in Russia, Nigeria, and Brazil are drinking more on average than their female counterparts in the United States.[1] These findings may indicate the pressure women feel to network within the existing cultural structure.

Early in her career, Mexican Xiomy Ricardo was the first woman to join the sales department at her multinational company. It was common for the men in her industry to have meetings during which they could drink tequila from 2 PM to 6 PM, every day. In many regions, a woman having lunch or a cup of coffee or tea—let alone drinks or dinner—with men would not be viewed favorably. But Xiomy knew she needed to build relationships with clients even if she found it unacceptable to participate in the afternoon drinking meetings. At first she participated in the meetings, but they made her uncomfortable and she found that not much actual business was being conducted. Undeterred, she changed her approach and decided to quit going to these meetings. "Instead I only scheduled sales breakfast meetings."

That tactic proved effective. It allowed Xiomy to meet and get to know her clients in a way that worked for her. "You have to work hard, network, show yourself, and sell yourself," she said.

Even in countries where female-male interactions must be carefully navigated many approaches to networking can work. Undeterred women can:

- Make appointments to meet people in their offices or at their own offices.
- Participate in networking events or conferences where there will be many people.
- Ask female peers to join them at gatherings so that they are not the only woman in attendance.
- Provide feedback to their companies that holding evening gatherings in places where it is not appropriate for women to join in negatively affects their ability to build relationships and excel at work. They recommend that more gatherings be planned for work hours and held in the workplace.

- Connect with people online through LinkedIn, online groups created by and for members of their industry, by sending articles and ideas to people, and by asking people in their social networks questions via email.

NO MATTER WHAT, DON'T "NOT NETWORK"

Some women decide they are too busy to network. This is one of the biggest career mistakes I've seen women make. Building a network seems to be one of the first things that women stop in their work-life integration efforts. They fail to realize that building a network is part of their work. It's not an additional, if-or-when-I-have-time activity.

I can't tell you how many times clients and former clients have called me to tell me that they want or need to find a new job, or that they need to speak with someone about their business. They call in a panic, telling me that they've been so busy working that they don't have contacts with the people they now need to reach out to.

Here's just one example. After taking some time off after her company was sold, a former client decided to start looking for a job. She thought that she could reach out to a couple recruiters and have coffee with a few people she had not kept in touch with over the past few years and she'd get a job. I admired her confidence, but unfortunately it's not that easy. Getting the right job is all about knowing people who are connected to opportunities and who know about your abilities and can vouch for you. You cannot build a network overnight and you won't have a strong network if you only connect with people when you want something from them.

The time to build a network is when there's nothing you need.

The time to build a network is now and always—not when you have time, not later, and not when you need it most.

MENTORS AND MENTORING

One important goal in networking is to develop relationships with a few mentors. A mentor is someone who gives sound and relevant advice, often based on his or her experience.

Lucila Suarez Battan, a young entrepreneur from Argentina relayed her experience. "I have a mentor whose name is Adriana Felella. I met her while I was working at Movistar a few years ago. At first, she helped me express myself regarding my needs, so I could ask for what I wanted in the corporation and distinguish myself. Although she was an expert in strategic communications and worked by herself, she took some time to coach me. Adriana mentored me by asking me questions that helped me think about something from a different perspective. A year later, she suddenly became my boss and our relationship grew stronger." Because Lucila had a close relationship with Adriana, her boss understood and was supportive of Lucila's preferred work schedule, allowing her to lead an integrated life.

Lucila explained, "I'm a night person. Mornings really are my weak spot. I don't like taking public transportation during rush hour, so I planned to start my day late and finish it late as well. I would get to the office around 10:30 AM, or sometimes even 11:00 AM. Adriana did not mind my work schedule because she knew that this was what made me happy and productive. Once in a while, I was even permitted to work from home."

Lucila's mentor helped her to focus on her skills and to discover her passion, even if that ultimately would take Lucila away from Movistar. She said, "I had a senior coworker who tended only to give me little things to do. He would do all the work that brought more exposure. Adriana did not like this because she saw potential in me so, little by little, she started assigning me better tasks. She supported me when some teammates who were getting less important assignments started to speak about me behind my back."

She went on, "In big corporations there can be a lot of gossip. I had to learn how to deal with it and avoid the negative comments. I was working really hard and Adriana helped me realize I deserved everything good that was happening for me. I had earned it. So my self-confidence grew stronger. She also helped me strike a better balance between my personal life and my work life and take action on things that were holding me back."

Like they did for Lucila, the right mentoring relationships will accelerate your success. A mentor relationship is not established overnight, as it is built on trust and mutual interests. You might have a mentor for a long time or just for a short period. Regardless, the goals are the same: to learn from your mentor's experience and insights. I highly recommend that you find mentors at every stage of your career.

> ## TYPES OF MENTORS
>
> There is often a need for different types of mentors. There are three types with whom I recommend you try to establish a relationship.
>
> - **Type 1.** A mentor who is knowledgeable in your field or industry.
> - **Type 2.** A mentor who has insightful perspectives about what it takes to be professionally successful.
> - **Type 3.** A mentor who is younger than you and therefore has different, more recent knowledge or experience in your field—or in another area you'd like to learn more about. This type of mentor is often called a *reverse mentor*. People don't usually think that a younger, less experienced person can be their mentor, but these mentors are a very important part of keeping abreast and ahead of new developments.

WAYS TO ESTABLISH A RELATIONSHIP WITH A MENTOR

What traits should your mentors have? Look for people who see and understand your strengths and weaknesses, as well as your career or business aspirations and your specific goals. They also should be people who understand your field or the field you wish to work in. Most importantly, your mentors should want and be willing to invest time with you. A great mentor will encourage you and also give you very direct feedback about what you should be thinking about, doing, and not doing.

Through networking, Croatian entrepreneur Ana Kolarević found her mentor, Saša Cvetojević. As the founder of a local technology incubator, he was one of the people who first saw Ana's new business idea pitch. Hearing what she said, he believed the business had potential and decided he wanted to help her realize her vision. Ana was fortunate.

For many other women, it can be difficult and even rare to find and connect with the right mentor. About half the women I've spoken with don't have mentors, a situation that is similar to the findings of the December 2013 study of more than 300 women entrepreneurs in nine countries in Latin America commissioned by the Multilateral Investment Fund (MIF), a member of the Inter-American Development Bank (IDB) and conducted by EY.[2]

Women like Ana Sanchez, a printed circuit board engineer for Intel in Guadalajara, Mexico, want mentors. She shared with me that although the various positions she has held throughout her career gave her technical skills, different points of view, and problem-solving capabilities, she wished she had a mentor to help her develop a career plan that would take her beyond her current job.

I asked Argentine business advisor Carolina Dams, who researches entrepreneurship, why so many women entrepreneurs *don't* have mentors. Her answer went beyond general assumptions. "It does not surprise me that most of the women do not have mentors. However, I believe it is not a gender issue. My guess is that if you ask men about it, you will get a similar answer. I believe the availability of mentoring is a cultural thing, and uncommon in this part of the world." She concluded, "Having a formal business mentor is a relatively new practice in Latin America."

Establishing a mentoring relationship takes time to evolve naturally. Most typically, a mentor will choose you. Sometimes, the two of you will mutually develop a relationship that results in mentoring. It is not appropriate or advisable to ask someone whom you have just met or only briefly met a few times to become your mentor.

You will most likely find your prospective mentor through your networking efforts. This is another reason why you need to network. As you meet people who you find insightful and from whom you think you can learn, reach out to them either in person, by phone, or via email, whichever is most appropriate. Let them know that you enjoyed meeting them and talking with them, and found their insights helpful. Then ask for their point of view or advice on a specific topic. Close by thanking them and asking what you can do to help them in return. Many people (I'm one) don't appreciate it when someone asks for advice and then never follows up with a note regarding what happened in the situation with which they needed help. So be sure to follow up to thank them, and specifically let them know how you used or benefited from their input. After following up, think of a way to reach out to your prospective mentor again this time with something interesting to share, such as an article, an event, or some useful information.

The next time you see your prospective mentor, spend a little time speaking with him or her and see if there is still a mutual connection. If so, ask this individual if he or she would be willing to meet with you to discuss a specific topic. If the prospective mentor agrees and the conversation goes well, follow up again with a quick update on what happened as a result of that discussion. Only after having had a few such interactions is it appropriate to ask the person if he or she would be willing to continue to guide you occasionally.

If the mentor agrees, ask how frequently and in what manner the mentor would prefer such interactions take place. As you continue to connect, follow up, and reach out with return value, some people may effectively become your mentors without you ever asking the question "Will you be my mentor?" As you refer to your mentor, you can use the term *mentor*, and your mentor will know the value you place on the advice you have been given.

Lovely Kumar, Chief of Projects at Larks Learning, a training and psychometric assessment company in India, described how she views the benefits of the mentoring she has received, "Every interaction is a learning opportunity and needs to be treated like that. As I look at my career, I can see various inflection points created by the many men and women who invested in me. What's interesting is that *none of these relationships developed through planned mentoring programs*, they were done in tiny slivers of time, like over a cup of coffee, while waiting for a meeting, and so on. As one of my mentors, M.M. Pant, says, 'When we meet, what I learn from you is mine. And what you learn from me is yours. That is the rule in a knowledge economy.'"

For women, there are may be additional challenges if the right mentor for them is a man—and often this will be the case. Don't let other people's potential perceptions stop you from establishing a relationship with a mentor.

DEALING WITH GENDER-RELATED MENTORING CONSTRAINTS

As more women enter and progress in the workforce, there are more women ready to be mentors. However, it is still very likely that your ideal mentor will be a man. Depending on where you live, this could raise a whole new set of challenges. How can you establish a mentoring relationship with a man without stressing cultural norms? In some countries, that will be a significant hurdle. But if the most appropriate mentor for you happens to be a man, take advantage of his counsel.

I asked men in growth economies what women could do to preempt people who would critically or unfairly judge a male-female mentoring relationship. They advised that women take the initiative to communicate very clearly and on a regular basis both internally within their organizations and externally in their communities about the nature of the meetings they are having with their mentors.

Olu Omoyele from Nigeria, who is a technical specialist at the Bank of England, said that he tells women that if they develop and maintain a consistent image, a strong sense of self, and project a business-focused identity, they will minimize opportunities for gossip and speculation about their relationships with their mentors. Omoyele also cautioned against women believing that they need more mentoring than they actually do. "Although ambitious women should seek mentoring, they should be careful not to be sucked in by the mindset that 'women need extra help,' because that is false."

Here are a few ways you can take cultural considerations into account.

- Have someone who is a mutual connection of both you and your prospective mentor approach the prospective mentor on your behalf.
- Meet your mentor only at his office or at your office and during business hours.
- Talk predominantly by phone, Skype, or email, rather than meeting in person. All over the world people have mentors who don't live in the same city, and they are still able to get the relevant advice they need.
- Speak with your company about the possibility of them creating a company-sponsored mentoring program so that your mentorship can be assigned to you, sanctioned by your employer, and not something you enter into on your own.

If the above options are not viable and you feel that it would not be permissible or appropriate for you to have a male mentor, and you can't find a woman who would be a good fit for your needs, don't be deterred or give up. There are some alternatives.

MENTORING ALTERNATIVES

Here are a few alternative methods for getting the mentoring you need.

Form an informal business advisory board. Identify a small group of people who have expertise in different topics that will help you to start or grow your business. Ask each individual if they would be willing to serve on a team of advisors to you and your business. Convene and meet with this group regularly to solicit their input and advice. As you grow your business, these individuals may later become part of a more formal board of directors. You will want to check into any legal ramifications regarding such a group. Also, assure potential advisory board members that they have no personal legal liability for the activities of your company.

Form a business or professional roundtable or peer-mentoring group. Identify a group of peers whose expertise and success you admire. You could include only women or both men and women. Members of the group would meet on a regular basis and mentor each other by sharing ideas, best practices, and contacts, and holding each other accountable for results.

Participate in remote mentoring. Research, identify, and apply for mentoring programs in which working women (both those who work in companies, and entrepreneurs) are paired with mentors in other cities or locations. Two exemplary programs of this kind for women in growth economies are offered by Cherie Blair Foundation and TechWomen.

Engage with thought partners. Identify individuals similar to those with whom you might engage through an advisory board or a professional roundtable, but in this case, meet with them individually rather than in a group—and on an as-needed versus a regular basis.

Participate in mentoring events. Businesswomen's organizations around the world hold in-person mentoring events where you can get advice on business issues you are grappling with from someone who is a volunteer mentor. This is not the same as having an ongoing relationship with a committed mentor, but you may meet someone at one of these events with whom you could develop such a relationship. One great example of these types of events is the Mentoring Walk organized around the world by Vital Voices.

Hire a business or career coach. If you have the resources to do so, hire a professional business coach or career coach who has the expertise to help you accomplish your objectives.

BE A MENTOR

In addition to having mentors, I also recommend that you make time to mentor someone yourself, perhaps another woman. Alena Vladimirskaya, founder of the recruiting company PRUFFI, in Russia, does just that. "It's not about being successful yourself, but about helping young talent grow, and to change the world for the better by helping businesses. I think females are the ones that take more responsibility, are eager to grow and learn, and take opportunities. That is why most of the people I hire at PRUFFI are women."

Here's how Alena's mentoring helped Sasha Olenina, founder of We Study In, develop her own company and navigate the entrepreneurial and venture capital landscape in Moscow. "I like raising young talent. Sasha asked for my support, my help, and knowledge, and I helped her to grow as a leader and entrepreneur." With Alena's help and mentorship, Sasha was able to raise US$300,000 in venture capital in Moscow to fund her startup company.

Asked what her relationship with Alena was like for her, Sasha said, "Alena found my profile on VK.com and messaged me. At that time, I had 50,000 followers on a scholarships and financial aid page for study abroad on VK. I started We Study In while I was in London. After a month, I relocated to Moscow, where Alena and I started to meet up and talk regularly. Alena helped me find the chief technology officer for my project. She also advised me on my marketing and used her contacts on my behalf. When we needed to approach someone she knew, such as our investor, the cofounder of HeadHunter (hh.ru), where Alena used to work, who brought money, skills, and knowledge, Alena would introduce us."

In Africa, Angela Oduor also mentors women. "During the launch of iHub in 2010, I realized that there were very few women in the room," Angela said. Only 15 percent of women in Kenya work in tech. "So, I cofounded AkiraChix, an organization that works to develop young women in technology, Our aim in founding AkiraChix was to create an avenue to encourage and mentor young women to take up careers in tech, and to help them be confident in the fact that they actually can succeed in the field. We mentor high school girls as well as university students, and introduce them to career opportunities in tech."

She continued, "We train young women from poor socioeconomic backgrounds, offering them a free one-year intensive course, and hope that by the end of the course they can use some of the skills they've gained to improve their economic situation. We also hold networking events to help women in the tech industry get to know each other and collaborate."

A SPONSOR

There is one more relationship that is essential if you want to accelerate your professional success, and that is to have a sponsor. A sponsor is someone who has the seniority, stature, and power to advocate for you. They use their influence to create more business or career opportunities for you.

Again, it is a lot simpler for men in growth economies (in fact for men anywhere in the world) to have a sponsor relationship, and today more men than women have sponsors. Like men, however, women need sponsors to get ahead. When women—when you—have a sponsor, opportunities for advancement increase. Having a sponsor is one of the career strategies that can make the most material difference in a woman's career advancement.

Because some women around the world are still unfamiliar with the term *sponsor*, I am going to define it. A sponsor is someone who has significant influence in your organization, industry, or market, who by purposefully advocating for you creates opportunities that accelerate your success. The term *sponsor* is most typically used to refer to an influential advocate within a company, but a sponsor can also be someone outside a company who has the desire and ability to help an entrepreneur.

Tantaswa Fubu, Executive head of People at KPMG in South Africa, is an active sponsor. "I identify female employees whom I believe have potential and appoint myself as their career sponsors, in most instances without formally discussing it with them. Whenever I have interesting and difficult projects, I make sure that I expose them to these projects so that they get to gain self-confidence in their own capabilities. I make them believe in their decision-making capabilities by refusing to make the decisions that pertain to their jobs for them. They need to make their own mistakes and learn from them. They need to feel empowered. I believe my role is to empower and support them.

"I am unfortunately, quite hard and demanding on people, but mostly they understand and appreciate where I want to take them and see that I truly have their best interests at heart. Also, this is about having critical conversations with our menfolk about trying to change the landscape, as we realize we cannot do this on our own."

In the Middle East, as in much of the world, the field of information technology (IT) is still largely known as a male-dominated field. But that didn't stop an undeterred Jordanian woman, Tamara Abdel Jaber. In 1997, when she was only twenty-six years old, Tamara founded an IT company and at the time of our interview, employed twenty-two full-time employees and 150 contractors across the Middle East. In 2011, *Arabian Business* magazine named her one of the 100 most powerful Arab women. Her company, Palma Consulting, has been recognized as one of the thirty fastest-growing companies in Jordan. Tamara attributes much of her confidence and success to the guidance she received from her sponsor, Khaled Kilani.

She shared, "I met Khaled right after I graduated from university. He saw my passion for entrepreneurship and my desire to start my own business. He promised me that after working with him for five years, I would be able to start my own business. Five years to the date, Palma was established. During the time I worked for Khaled, I got to work on lots of companies and lead many investments. I was exposed to legal issues, taxation, and human resources, adding these skills to my educational base in business, finance, accounting, and IT. The knowledge and experience I gained gave me the courage to start my own business."

Some people argue that a sponsor is more important than a mentor. My opinion is that both are equally important relationships for different reasons; and either can be more important at different career stages. Early in your career and during times of career or business transition, the right kind of mentor or coach is invaluable. A mentor shares experience and provides feedback and critical advice to help you process situations and figure out your best course of action.

On the other hand, you need a sponsor when there is a specific professional goal you want to reach. When you know which opportunity you want or when there are assignments, projects, or business opportunities that would be invaluable to your career or business (whether you know about them or not), a sponsor can help you get them.

THE DIFFERENCES BETWEEN MENTORS AND SPONSORS

Here's a quick way to see and understand the differences between a mentor and a sponsor.

MENTORS ...	SPONSORS ...
Give you their time.	Give you opportunities.
Work with you in private.	Work for you in public.
Invest in you.	Make investments for you.
Help you change.	Make change happen for you.
Give you advice.	Advocate for you and give you their endorsement.

Sometimes working with a mentor results in a lot of good activity—talking, encouragement, and advice—but it does not help you get what you want. The purpose of a sponsor is to get results. Successful working women know that promotions are not predicated on performance alone, and the best assignments don't always go to the *most deserving* (however this term is defined in your company). Successful businesswomen also know that although both mentors and sponsors are key components of their career strategy, the right sponsor can make the difference between stagnation and progress.

I spent sixteen years at Bank of America. It was my first job after graduate school. I started as a commercial lender and had a wonderful career with lots of growth and opportunities. I worked hard. I produced results. Being from the Middle East, having lived and traveled around the world, and speaking several languages brought me early opportunities in international banking and visibility in the organization. Bank of America was growing rapidly at the time and the bank had a wonderful practice of cross-developing talent by placing people in jobs they had no prior experience or background in.

I was fortunate to have my contributions and potential recognized by leaders at the bank, so I had several job rotations. The first of these was managing the bank's management training program in the Mid-Atlantic region of the United States. Then I was moved to a position in the Organization Development and Training department. Successive moves ultimately resulted in a role managing training, development, and executive education for the Virginia bank. While my results, my managers, and mentors played significant roles in my career trajectory, exposure to the key decision-makers who could influence my career came after the Virginia bank president, Doug Cruickshanks, gave me some challenging assignments and treated me as his partner. His sponsorship proved invaluable to me.

WAYS TO FIND A SPONSOR

If you want to get a sponsor, focus on producing the results that senior, influential business leaders will notice. Sponsors typically choose the people they want to champion, not the other way around. They choose people based on what they see and know of their capabilities, contributions, and future potential. Some leading-edge organizations create formal sponsorship programs to facilitate career assignments for high-potential employees. If you work for such an organization, then your job is to produce results and be visible so you can be assigned an influential sponsor.

If you are an entrepreneur, if your organization does not have such a program, or if you have not been tapped to be a part of such a program, you should do your best to identify your own sponsor.

Sponsors put their reputation on the line to advocate for someone. To be able to advocate for you, a sponsor has to be able to communicate your achievements and aspirations. In order for a sponsor to communicate your achievements, the sponsor has to know what these are. So remember to make your results known.

It is not typical to ask someone to be your sponsor. The process works more like this:

- As you deliver results and make your achievements known, you will come to the attention of influential leaders.
- Initially, your role is to add value to *them* and *their* businesses.
- As you add value, you will start building a relationship that gives you the platform for sharing your aspirations.
- At this point, you can begin to ask for their help in getting you involved in a specific job or project you want.
- Express your openness to taking assignments that potential sponsors may bring to your attention.
- Express your intent to perform at the highest level in every situation, and your commitment to a future at the company.
- As you help influential leaders, they may decide to further advocate for you and become your sponsors.

For more on the role of a sponsor, I recommend Sylvia Hewlett's book: *Forget a Mentor, Find a Sponsor: The New Way to Fast Track Your Career.*

NOW IT'S YOUR TURN

Use the following self-reflection activities and action steps to improve your network.

⟨?⟩ SELF-REFLECTION: WHAT'S THE QUALITY OF YOUR NETWORK?

Assess your network in the following ways.

- Do I have a deep and broad network, a limited network, or a small-to-nonexistent network? Use the Up, Down, In, and Out framework to evaluate how many people and the type of people you are connected with.

- How frequently and in what manner do I connect with the people in my network?

- What are my preferred and most comfortable ways to network?
  Examples: At events, one on one, online.

ACTIONS
TO STRENGTHEN YOUR NETWORK

Take the following actions to broaden and deepen your network.

- Based on your career or business goals, identify three to five people you'd like to connect with or with whom you'd like to renew contact.

- Based on your preferred style of networking, identify where your best chances of connecting with your targets are—and how to do so.

- Make a plan with a specific time to reach out and connect with the people you have identified.

⦵ SELF-REFLECTION: WHAT KIND OF MENTORING ARE YOU GIVING AND GETTING?

Evaluate your mentoring.

- Am I getting the type of mentoring and advice I need to help me achieve success as I define it?

- How often do my mentors and I meet?

- Am I mentoring anyone?

- How often do I meet with the people I'm mentoring?

⦵ ACTIONS TO ELEVATE YOUR GUIDANCE

Remember that maintaining and strengthening your network takes attention and effort. You may need to make changes to your schedule or priorities in order to get the type of mentoring or sponsorship you want.

- If you are getting the type of mentoring you need, express your gratitude to your mentors and share with them how their guidance is helping you.

- If you feel that you need additional guidance, identify someone from your network who you believe would be helpful to you, go back to the section in this chapter on establishing a relationship with a mentor and develop a plan to establish a relationship with them.

- If you are already a mentor, commend yourself for the guidance you are providing.

- If you are not yet a mentor, identify someone you can help, and begin a relationship with them.

SELF-REFLECTION: ARE YOU READY FOR A SPONSOR?

If you are ready to take your career or business to the next level you would likely benefit from having a sponsor. Evaluate whether you are ready for a sponsor by asking the following questions.

- Am I a strong performer who consistently works on her professional development, and who shows initiative in taking on new work assignments?

- Do I make significant contributions and create results for my organization?

- Am I known by this potential sponsor and well thought of by him or her? Ways to become known include volunteering to work on projects, committees, initiatives, and/or community activities that the potential sponsor is leading and is passionate about.

- Do I know how I'd like my career to develop and what sorts of future roles I'd like to take? Can I articulate my desires to my potential sponsor?

If you answered yes to the questions above, take the following actions to connect with a potential sponsor.

ACTIONS
TO HELP YOU CONNECT WITH A
POTENTIAL SPONSOR

If you can answer yes to all of the above questions, then on your own or through a mentor, begin to build a relationship with a senior leader at your organization or in your industry at large who has the power and influence to serve as your sponsor. If you cannot answer yes to all five questions, continue to improve your skills and results. Then, carefully cultivate a relationship with people in your network as outlined earlier.

SUMMARY

Building your professional network and having mentors and sponsors helps you get the opportunities that lead to success as you have defined it. Use what you know, your contacts, and the contributions you make to seek out opportunities. There are ample opportunities available for women with education, skills, confidence, and drive.

To supercharge your success, your career or business advancement plan should include:

- A strong network with four types of connections: up (more senior people), down (more junior people), in (your organization), and out (people in your field and community).
- Mentoring.
- Gaining opportunities through your own initiative and perhaps through the support of a sponsor.

NOTES

— HABIT 6 —

Lead

*Create new paths for
yourself and others.*

I AM BOTHERED WHEN I HEAR WOMEN BEING TOLD
they *should* get to the "next level" or "scale" their businesses,
that they should not to be satisfied with running a small business,
but should "think big." This type of talk goes against my belief
that women are entitled to their own definitions of success, so
I won't take that approach here. I'm not going to tell you that
you should necessarily strive for an executive position or to start
or grow your own business, unless these are things you want
for yourself. At the same time, I'd be delighted and fully ready
to support you if these were your goals. I support each woman
focusing on achieving her personal definition of success.

The principle that I do advocate is that you *lead*. I encourage
you to think of yourself as someone with the leadership ability to

be a role model and to make a difference. Leading is the habit of creating new paths for yourself and others. It will take leadership to do more than clear obstacles and to drive economic prosperity. It will take changing systems, practices, traditions, laws, and deeply held beliefs to eliminate gender equality barriers once and for all.

You've been leading your whole life since you were on the playground, in your home, and in your workplace. You might not have always recognized or seen yourself as a leader, and you might not have known when others were looking to you for leadership, but I assure you, you've been in this role throughout your life. The only question is this: Where do you want to go with the innate leader inside of you?

Our world needs leaders. Your country needs leaders. Your community needs leaders. For an economy to grow and a nation to develop, it needs to engage all the bright, talented people it has. It needs its entire population to address and resolve the opportunities and the problems of the day. It needs you.

People in growth economies are already leading in different ways. A Grant Thornton study of 3,500 business leaders in forty-five economies found that there are two distinct styles of leaders: modernists and traditionalists. Modernist leaders are more open to drawing on their intuition and creative instincts, while traditionalist leaders rank intuition and creativity as less important skills. The study found that emerging markets like Brazil, Thailand, the Philippines, and Vietnam have a prevalence of modernist leaders, while traditionalist leaders were generally found in European economies such as those of France, Germany, Spain, and the United Kingdom.[1]

Even more interestingly Francesca Lagerberg, a global leader at Grant Thornton, concluded, "Business leaders in Asia and Latin America have been able to observe how management techniques in the West have evolved and matured. The research shows, however, that rather than simply copying and replacing management techniques, they are blending them with their own cultural and management practices to adopt a 'third way' for their local market. In my opinion, the fact that business leaders in these economies are more likely to be women is not a coincidence. They appear to show greater openness to coaching, place greater emphasis on more modern management techniques, and are also more willing to delegate. We're definitely seeing a difference of approach that highlights the value to business of having gender diversity in senior roles."[2]

Undeterred women begin by leading themselves down the paths they've identified and chosen. They stay on the path until they adapt whatever they're doing to develop solutions that work well for them, their colleagues, and their clients. Because their goals are meaningful to them, they persevere. Their desire to actualize their visions gets them out of bed every morning with enthusiasm, ready to take on the day. Leaders know how to marshal their energy so they do not waste effort.

Everything you've reflected on and put into practice while reading this book has made you even more ready than you already were to lead—yes, *lead*—the life you want to live. To lead is to have a vision, to innovate and to find solutions. Leading is not only about clearing the obstacles that hinder you, it's also about making the changes that result in real solutions and more opportunities.

It's hopeful.

It's where you add value.

NOTES

FORGE
A NEW
PATH

CHAPTER 10

CHANGE

You are the solution.

I F YOU'RE THE WOMAN I KNOW YOU ARE, YOU'VE created new paths for yourself and others throughout your life. You may be among the first women in your family to go to college, get a master's degree or a Ph.D., or to study abroad. You may be among the first women in your family to have a corporate career or hold a senior management position. You may be among the first women in your community to have started or grown a business, or to have led a community organization, engaged in a charitable venture, or served on a board of directors. Perhaps you serve on a corporate board. Perhaps you are a CEO. Likely you are also a role model to girls and other women. If any of these descriptions fit you, you are already a leader.

After reading this book, you are even more ready and set to accelerate your success than you were before. You're in action. Your confidence, courage, and contributions enable you to lead. Take this opportunity to decide where and how you want to continue to lead. What direction do you want to take your leadership in?

As someone who has worked in management and leadership development, coaching leaders for over twenty-six years, there are a few leadership experts whose views resonate with me and inform my work. Since my early career, James Kouzes and Barry Posner, authors of *The Leadership Challenge*, which has been one of the top bestselling business books for more than twenty-five years, have been two of my favorites. Their conclusion about leadership is: "Leadership is not the private reserve of a few charismatic men and women. It is a process that ordinary people use when they are bringing forth the best from themselves and others."[1] And so it is with you, me, and the women featured in *Undeterred*, ordinary women who seek to bring out the best in themselves and others.

WAYS WOMEN LEAD

In addition to having an undeterred attitude, the women from growth economies whom I interviewed, researched, and analyzed all had an area in which they led—some in small ways, others in large ways, but always leaving some situation better than they found it. Undeterred women don't let stereotypes of what a leader looks like or acts like dictate the way they lead.

They lead by developing innovative products, enabling other women, working in male-dominated fields, and taking on formal leadership roles.

Developing innovating product or services. Some women, like entrepreneurs Afnan Ali in Jordan and Mary Anne de Amorim Ribeiro in Brazil, envisioned and created new products to meet unmet needs.

An electrical engineer, Afnan invented a personal mobile heating device called TEPLO. Mary Anne packaged a set of playful activities designed to stimulate the cognitive development of children—CDs of infant songs, books, LEGO® kits, and other toys—with guides explaining their use, and put them into the hands of parents of children under the age of six in the approximately twelve million low-income families in her country who lacked access to formal daycare centers or preschools.

Other leaders, like entrepreneurs Regina Agyare in Ghana, Sasha Olenina in Russia, Denise Abulafia in Argentina, and Ana Kolarević in Croatia, found new and innovative ways to solve real issues and market needs in their own countries.

Through her technology company, Soronko Solutions, Regina sparked social change. She developed a location-based mobile app for small and medium-sized enterprises in Accra, which helps those businesses gain visibility and compete against bigger businesses. Her company also engages in social projects, such as teaching math, science, and engineering to kids in rural areas of Ghana. Sasha's company, We Study In, provides opportunities for teens to study internationally.

Denise Abulafia's organization, Educatina, has produced over 3,000 educational videos and serves on average more than 300,000 students per month. Educatina reaches and inspires students to learn by using modern teaching approaches and online videos and course work.

In Croatia, Ana oversaw the development of the Sizem system, which properly measures a woman's bust and recommends the right bra sizes for her from the comfort of her home. All consumers have to do to use it is to type their measurements into the website or app and they are linked to the stores that sell the intimate apparel they want.

Enabling other women. You would probably agree that these examples of leadership through innovation are evident. But there are countless other types of leaders, including women who lead in order to help other women. For instance, in addition to running the human resources consulting firm Altavis Pvt Ltd., Sarika Bhattacharyya cofounded the online network BizDivas, a community where professional women in India help one another advance their careers and lives. Her reason? "We want to help increase the participation of women in the Indian economy at all levels. We would like to see a corporate environment conducive to the growth of professional women with more flexible work options. We want to see more women in the boardroom."

Similarly, in Brazil, senior IT leader Sandra Portugal operates a website called Projetando Pessoas that encourages women's professional development.

As part of running her steel and aluminum welding company, South African business owner Tebogo Mashego has the opportunity to travel and attend world-class professional development programs. She makes copies of materials she is provided in these programs, gives them to women with no access to the Internet, and hosts discussions in her home to pass on what she has learned at events she has attended.

Argentinian Maria Gabriella Hoch works as a volunteer through the NGO Vital Voices to provide leadership to expand networking, mentoring, and professional development opportunities for women in Argentina. Several other Argentinian women I met are also committed to helping businesswomen. Lorena Diaz mentors women within her far-reaching professional network. Silvia Torres Carbonell teaches entrepreneurship and is known as one the foremost leaders on women entrepreneurs in Argentina. Marta Cruz enables women entrepreneurs to succeed through NXTP Labs, the business accelerator she cofounded.

In Kuwait, Rania Azmi, Ph.D., an investment and finance adviser to a major Middle East sovereign wealth fund, is also a tireless advocate for women with breast cancer.

To explain her own motivation to be helpful to other women, South African Tantaswa Fubu said, "Knowing that I have positively impacted someone and left her at a better space than I found her gives me a great sense of accomplishment. I live for this."

Working in fields previously dominated by men. Many women are now leading in fields that have traditionally been populated almost exclusively by men. These pioneers include women like Nisreen Ahmed Jaffer, the first female petroleum engineer in Oman; Russian venture capitalist Lyubov Simonova; manufacturers Tebogo Mashego in South Africa and Yvonne Chow in China; and Jordanian Afnan Ali, whose career is in engineering and robotics. There are also a whole host of others who work in technology, including Divine Ndhlukula from Zimbabwe, who said that the way she succeeded in the male-dominated field of security with "next to nothing in capital and no security background" was by seeing a gap in the marketplace that others did not.[2]

Nigerian Adeshola Komolafe, founder of Media Insight, described her experience. "The world is male-dominated. At the beginning, it was tough being a woman in a male-dominated industry. My firm was up against well-established firms. In some cases, they even had prior relationships with our target clients. We were the underdogs. Couple this with the fact that the firm was led by a woman! The only way to beat the competition was to be innovative. To compete effectively, we had to be way better than our competition. So we researched the latest trends and studied our prospective clients. We reviewed their past attempts, and worked out ways to offer them better services at cheaper rates. Our competition could not compete with our new strategy of offering better services at cheaper rates.

"To keep our overhead down, we outsourced nonessential services. We encouraged our clients to give us endorsement letters to show that they were satisfied with our services. Then we used these letters in our future marketing efforts, acting as a springboard to get clients who otherwise might not have considered us."

Taking on formal leadership roles. More women are leading from senior positions in their organizations. More women are leading by starting their own businesses. More women are demonstrating leadership by advocating for people in need in their communities. You've read about them throughout the book and maybe you are one of them yourself.

Undeterred women are leaders and role models in their families, in their communities, in their workplaces, and in their professions—even globally. As you reflect on these women's experiences, ask yourself how these women demonstrate different types of leadership and how you want to lead.

PREPARE YOURSELF TO LEAD

As with other habits, the habit of leading starts inside, with your own thoughts and beliefs. Leaders like you and the undeterred women mentioned in this book view the future with optimism and energy. In his book *The One Thing You Need to Know*, Gallop Organization senior researcher Marcus Buckingham says (changing all pronouns to the feminine), "Great leaders rally people to a better future. . . . What defines a leader is her preoccupation with the future. In her head she carries a vivid image of what the future could be, and this image drives her on."[3] I want to underscore the word *better*, because it represents the optimism of leaders. Leaders are essentially forward thinkers who believe that an unlimited number of innovations, ideas, and improvements are possible—unlimited ways to improve their own performance and to make situations better. To be a leader, start by envisioning a better future. Take the initiative to generate ideas, be resourceful, and innovate or make improvements to create the results you envision.

If this type of optimistic thinking is common in advanced economies, it should be doubly so in growth economies where there are even more opportunities for leadership.

For women, the strength to lead also comes from understanding and valuing the special perspective and talents that only women bring to the table. Although articles, books, and training sessions are filled with directives to women to act "more like men" in the workplace, I've never understood this advice. What would be the value in that? Instead, women should capitalize on the strengths and insights they bring, contribute in their unique ways, and expand their economies for the better.

Personally, I think about succeeding as a woman in business this way. To win a game, you have to know what game you are playing and the rules of the game. To succeed in business, you have to understand the industry you are in and how things work in that field. Once you know what the game is and what the rules are, you don't need to play the game like everyone else does (like all your competitors). It is best to develop your own strategy and play your position your way. And if you don't like the game or the rules of the game, you always have the option to create a new game with new rules, as long as you have the ideas and resources to do so, and as long as you can lead others to come join you.

In business, your role is to understand the game you're playing and to bring your strengths and talents to the table. If those strengths include what are traditionally thought of us "female characteristics" —traits like communication and collaboration—then great, bring them. Those are likely not strengths the majority of the other players (read: *men*) have.

Nisreen Ahmed Jaffer talked about her role as the first female petroleum engineer in Oman and how her ability to lead a team led to her success. "Back then, there were very few qualified Omani male engineers, let alone female engineers," Nisreen said. "This, in my view, is one of the early evidences of the country's effective leadership vision for female empowerment in Oman. In those days, in a male-dominated society, it was always a challenge for a woman to be recognized and to be accepted as a colleague or as a boss. I had to really prove myself in my job."

Nisreen continued to prove herself and advance in her career, ultimately becoming Director General of Promotion Investment at Oman's Public Authority for Investment Promotion & Export Development. "The challenges were many," Nisreen said. "Internally, my team was young and inexperienced. There were many external stakeholders, and securing their full cooperation and understanding was required. Engaging them was the key to attracting more investments in Oman."

Last, leaders understand that every person can lead, that you don't have to be in a special "leadership position" to have the authority to lead. Any woman can lead from whatever position she is in. In fact, all of the more than 250 women I connected with as I researched this book are leaders!

Here's Michelle Wang talking about the innovation that young Chinese leaders like her are bringing to their endeavors. "What I can comment a little on is the topic of young women in China, like me, who've had overseas educational experiences. An interesting, but also natural trend is that many of them have brought a western influence into their fields of work in China, oftentimes taking an entrepreneurial approach. These are not the 'groundbreaking innovations' people usually talk about, but these leaders are considered innovative in China due to their new ways of thinking and approaching business.

"For example, the study abroad consulting industry in China has mostly focused on preparing students for TOEFL and SAT tests. Having encountered both educational systems in China and the United States, my friend Odele thought Chinese students needed more help in developing their independent thinking skills to better adapt to the western university environment, so she set up her own training institute, CYPA, where Chinese high school students are given the opportunity to experience western ways of teaching for a year before they enter universities in the United States. This kind of innovative approach is particularly important for a startup environment, because it not only helps to differentiate a company from its competitors, but it is also much easier to help formulating the corporate DNA at the early stage."

TO LEAD, STEP INTO ACTION

The habit of leading is not just about thinking like a leader; it is about acting like a leader. It involves taking personal responsibility and concrete steps to change things for the better and seizing opportunities in new ways to make improvements for the future.

Here's how Denise Abulafia, the visionary Argentine entrepreneur who founded Educatina, the education company that is upending how students are taught, did it. Denise has a doctorate in biochemistry. "I taught for five years at a university in Mexico, the first few at a medical school. I was told that my students were not motivated and did not want to go to school, and that they didn't believe they could do something in the future with what they were learning. Since I was a researcher and it's in my nature to experiment, I created a lot of experiments to get them engaged and motivated. Then, I let them use computers in class. I was the only professor who let them use computers, laptops, and tablets while I was teaching. All the other teachers prohibited such use in class, but I allowed it. It was very challenging because by searching online, the students were able to ask me very difficult, very challenging questions while I was teaching. But I enjoyed it. I would say, 'I have no idea! Let's go look it up!' Then, 'Now that we have that information, let's analyze it!'

"We did a lot of fun projects. I made them form their own virtual company, and they had to do a lot of research, write a business plan, and sell it. It worked very nicely! The virtual company was in the medical sector—I was teaching proteomics—the study of proteins (such as how you create insulin). Doctors don't usually care about proteomics; they just want to do surgery on patients. What I learned was that the students were actually interested, that they were actually motivated, that they did want to learn. They just didn't want to be taught the way students have been taught for many years—by a teacher standing in the front of the room lecturing at them. They were bored. They wanted to be engaged. They wanted to interact. So, we needed to change the way we taught students so they could learn.

"What I know is education, and I know how to make things happen. Fixing the education model is something that is very complicated, not only in Argentina, but also in the rest of the world. We have to change things step by step."

NOW IT'S YOUR TURN

Whether you would like to lead by developing new products and services, by improving existing systems, by heading a business or community initiative, or by committing yourself to one-on-one relationships, you can identify excellent opportunities to lead by observing, listening, and gathering information. Then be undeterred in sharing your vision or example for change.

⊘ SELF-REFLECTION: WHAT CAN YOU CHANGE?

To identify your opportunities to lead, ask yourself:

- What do I care most about?

- What can I influence or change?

- Is there a situation or issue that I can improve?

- What has not been thought of that should be considered?

- What has not been done that should be done?

- What changes do I or others think are needed?

- Where are there unmet needs?

- What could be done better?

- What are the direction and strategy of the company where I work?

- What is important to my company's success?

- What is the biggest influence on my company's profitability?

- What do the CEO and executive management team care most about?

- What do the customers care most about?

ACTIONS
TO BRING ABOUT CHANGE

Take what you uncovered in your self-reflection and then:

- **Start where you are.**
  Think about what you know and what you are good at. Start from the role you are in. No matter what position you occupy, you *can* lead. You have the knowledge, information, and insights to make a difference.

- **Make connections from what you uncover.**
  This is where women have an advantage. We are good listeners, observers, and learners. Take the information you've been gathering and envision a new way or a better way.
  Examples: Identify problems, pain points, and opportunities. Bring ideas from one industry into another to provide fresh, new improvements. Bring experiences from situations that are similar to the situation you want to improve.

- **Speak up and propose ideas.**
  Examples: Be bold and specific in your proposal. Present your ideas in business language and explain how results can be measured. Use a combination of written material, images, and conversation to convey

*your leadership ability. Apply what you have seen
other effective leaders do in similar situations.*

- **Be an example of how you think something
  should be done.**
  If people are resistant to change or unwilling to do
  things in a new way, demonstrate leadership by doing
  what needs to be done in the new or better way.

- **Anticipate challenges and failures.**
  If you can anticipate what your challenges will be and
  who might challenge you, you can talk to people in
  advance, work to build support, and then make some
  adjustments in your approach that make it easier for
  your ideas to be heard and accepted. Making mistakes is
  okay if they help you do better the next time.

In our discussion about leadership, we have come full circle
from where we started at the beginning of the book. In Chapter
1, I explained that the main reason women in growth economies
succeed is because they clear obstacles. To clear obstacles, you
have to be undeterred by the things that come between you and
what you want to achieve. But to completely remove obstacles
so they are no longer there for you or anyone else requires
something more. It requires leadership to change systems and
challenge the status quo. To find lasting solutions, you have to
be innovative and resourceful. You have to lead.

SUMMARY

You become a leader as soon as you decide when, where, and how you want to lead. There will be times when you will see that you are the one who can solve a problem or create change that makes a difference. As you assume personal responsibility to make things better, you'll be leading.

As with other success habits, the habit of leading starts inside—with your own thoughts and beliefs—and requires bold action. Your leadership doesn't have to resemble a stereotyped image. Lead in your own way. Start by identifying opportunities for improvement and change. Lead by gathering information, thinking strategically about the future, proactively sharing your ideas and solutions. Lead from where you are and lead by your example.

CONCLUSION

You are the woman
the world has been waiting for.

A MEMORABLE MOMENT IN MY LIFE IS FROM A conversation with Becky Blades, a friend who is also part of my business network.

Becky has a hearing impairment. She grew up in a financially struggling household with six siblings in a poor, urban neighborhood in Kansas City, Missouri, in the middle of the United States of America. Lip-reading classes were not available at her neighborhood school, but they were offered in a school across town. In the eighth grade, she was allowed to change schools to take these classes.

To get to the new school, she rode a city bus. The route the bus went along was one of the loveliest parkways in the city, a road lined with many beautiful homes. Becky looked out the window of the bus during these daily trips to and from home, and one day she had a revelation. There wasn't just one big, beautiful house. There weren't just a few beautiful houses. There were blocks and blocks of beautiful houses. That meant there wasn't just one successful person (a fluke) . . . or only a few successful people who were born in the right place at the right time . . . no, there had to be many, many successful people. If so many people could be successful, then the odds were that she could be, too.

That insight was the seed of Becky's self-confidence. It was the moment when she first saw that opportunities were available to her. She went on to build a career in the public relations field, and to start, grow, and sell a business. She is a wife and a mother, an author, an accomplished artist, and an influential and generous leader in the arts and business community.

Just as the houses planted a seed in Becky's mind, Becky's story reminds me of the opportunities that are now available to educated, ambitious women in growth economies.

While some authors focus on the cultural, historical, or environmental difficulties of being a working woman in your country, I see this as a crucial and positive time for women. I believe that the next decade holds an unusual window of opportunity for women in growth economies.

As I showed in the Introduction, women's opportunities are opening up in countries where the business world has long been dominated by men. As growth economies rise in the global market, they need more skilled professionals and more leaders than ever before. Women can step into to these roles, meet these needs, and choose to pursue their own definitions of success. Because of the rise in demand and need for skilled workers, women have more access to jobs than ever before. Although achieving gender equality has been an intractable problem whose solution has eluded us for millennia, I believe that the path to parity in our workplaces will be cleared when each of us persistently takes the actions that accelerate our success.

My husband regularly reminds me—and his experience and results bear out his wisdom—that sustained success is primarily about execution; doing what needs to be done, when it needs to be done, doing it well, and doing it consistently. For successful women around the world, taking advantage of opportunities means working consistently and creatively.

Successful women in growth economies have six indelible habits. They are undeterred, prepared, and focused. They integrate their work into their lives, implement career acceleration strategies, and take every opportunity to lead. The women you read about in this book are *always* developing, honing, and implementing these success habits. Because they have these habits, undeterred women are in shape and have the muscle memory to be confident, courageous, and competent. Like Becky, undeterred women see the opportunities that could be theirs and they create plans to achieve the goals they envision. They courageously take their chances at the right moments with the habits that drive them toward success.

It is my deep desire that you achieve your version of success by embracing these habits for yourself. I hope the stories of women you've read about in this book have served to inspire you and that my coaching will guide you. Come back to them as you progress and encounter new challenges in your career or business. Each time, you will glean new insights and take away new ideas.

I have no doubt that you will achieve success as you envision it. All you have to do is start where you are and take consistent action toward what you desire. By stepping out as a leader, you will be able to help propel yourself forward. You are in the most optimal time and place to achieve what you want and to create a new future for yourself, your family, your country, and the world. Don't let anyone or anything keep you from taking advantage of the window of opportunity now before you.

Never forget, you are the woman the world has been waiting for!

Please send me an email at
raniaanderson@thewaywomenwork.com to share
how adopting these six success habits has influenced
your life and your work.

If you like, take a photo of yourself with *Undeterred*
or the companion workbook, *I Am Undeterred*, and
post it on your social networks. Use the hashtag
#IAMundeterred. I know I'll be inspired by your experience,
and I'd love to be able to share your example to inspire
and motivate other women around the world.

ACKNOWLEDGMENTS

WHEN I SET OUT TO TRANSFORM MY DREAM INTO this book, I had no idea what it took for an author to write and publish. There's an expression that it takes a village. In my case, it took a few continents.

It's impossible for me to convey the depth of my gratitude for those who supported and guided me on this journey. None more so than my husband, Lance, who was by my side through every step of the process. Through his words, and mostly through his example, he's been my inspiration to persevere and think big. The other man in my heart is my son, Nick. From him I learned about pursuing your own definition of success. I know beyond a shadow of a doubt that without the love of these two men none of this would be remotely possible.

What I learned repeatedly during this journey was never to lose faith in my mission and to trust that the right people and the resources I needed would be there when the time was right and I needed them the most; although they often showed up just in the nick of time and later than I hoped!

First, I met Erin Risner. Her title at The Way Women Work is Director of Community Engagement, but that role is just one small part of who she is to me. Erin has been my confidant, my supporter, my accountability partner, and my cheerleader. She's helped to build The Way Women Work community and brand. She's interviewed and corresponded with many undeterred women. She's challenged me to make tough decisions. She's been there for me when things got tough. We have a relationship in which we flow seamlessly from coworkers to deep friends.

After months of fits and starts with the manuscript, I realized that I didn't know how to write a book. It's not at all like writing anything else. My guide to figuring it out was Ishita Gupta. She taught me not only how to write a book but also how to get my dreams on paper. She helped me get unstuck and pushed me to tap into my heart as well as my head.

Another thing I didn't really understand at the beginning was what an editor does. It is so much more than my broadest expectation of the role. The first thing my editor, Stephanie Gunning, did was to get as deeply as she could into the mind of my readers. From that place, she went about restructuring my book so that the reader experience flowed smoothly. From thinking strategically to examining the use of every word, she was the best kind of partner I could have only imagined possible.

This book has been four years in the making. Along the way, dear friends never stopped believing in me. They listened as I recounted every high and low. They offered ideas and encouragement and accepted all the times I had to say no to getting together. I will be forever touched by the love and wisdom of Diane Power, Darcy Howe, Joann Schwarberg, Victoria Barnard, and Lynn Hinkle.

At the very early stages of writing this book, when I really had no idea what I was doing, I relied on Steff Hendenkamp, Jensen Power, and Carter Schwarberg to get started. Carter has been my design guide from the beginning. It is only fitting that she is the one who designed the book and workbook covers, which so perfectly embody the spirit of undeterred women.

When I needed help from authors who had actually completed and published books, I was welcomed with open arms by Becky Blades, Alana Mueller, and Diana Kander. They freely shared their lessons of experience. When I needed to know more about the book editing and publishing world, I turned to Reiko Davis, a young woman I had mentored to get a job in publishing and who now had the knowledge to mentor me. When I needed strategic thinking regarding marketing the book, Anita Newton generously shared her remarkable talent and ideas. The conviction of her belief in what I am doing inspired me even more to shoot for the stars. "Be audacious!" she said.

Three books in particular informed my thinking as I wrote *Undeterred*. These were *The Power of Habit* by Charles Duhigg, *Switch: How to Change Things When Change Is Hard* by Chip Heath and Dan Heath, and *Outliers: The Story of Success* by Malcolm Gladwell. The seminal works of these thought leaders helped me frame my message to future undeterred women.

Then there are the technical elements of getting a book published. Like every other person who appeared at the exact moment I needed them, I was introduced to Charlotte Cline-Smith at just the right time. A remarkable young woman, who grew up entirely in the developing world and who works with female university students from emerging economies, Charlotte proofed and edited the manuscript from the reader's perspective and handled the correspondence and database management that we couldn't proceed without.

Next, Andrew Pautler stepped in. He created the interior of this book and he is the design talent behind my websites. His calm, positive, never-ruffled approach, coupled with the speed that he gets work done, brought my words to life. For copyediting, I have Claire Putsche to thank; for proofing, Madelin Stone; for indexing, Andrea Jones; and for project and production management, the unfailing commitment and expertise once again of Stephanie Gunning at Lincoln Square Books.

I honor my mother, who was my first example of a strong woman and who worked until she was seventy-seven, and Beth K. Smith, whose lifelong example of empowering women one woman at a time fueled my goals.

At its core, this book was only made possible through the grace of more than 250 undeterred women who gave generously of their time, themselves, and their experiences—most especially the following eighty-six women. I am forever grateful to each and every one of you. Thank you for helping me make a positive difference in the world.

UNDETERRED WOMEN

Tamara Abdel Jaber

Denise Abulafia

Regina Agyare

Nisreen Ahmed Jaffer

Aisha Alfardan

Afnan Ali

Mary Anne de Amorim Ribeiro

Paula Arregui

Reem Asaad

Haifa Dia Al-Attia

Rania Azmi

Liheng Bai

Ritika Bajaj

Salwa Bamieh

Maisa Batayneh

Sarika Bhattacharyya

Irina Bullara

Jennifer Cheung

Yvonne Chow

Núbia Correia

Marta Cruz

Carolina Dams

Unmana Datta

Flavia De Hora

Aleksa Delsol

Lynn De Souza

Lorena Diaz

Esmat El Nahas

Neveen El Tahri

Shahira Fahmy

Azza Fawzi

Gordana Frgačić

Tantaswa Fubu

Maria Luisa Fulgueira

Yoanna Gouchtchina

Pooja Goyal

Polina Gushcha

Marta Harff

Maria Gabriela Hoch

Nour Jarrar

Maja Jelisic Cooper

Christine Khasinah-Odero

May Khoury

Ana Kolarević

Adeshola Komolafe

Taisiya Kudashkina

Lovely Kumar

Wee Yen Lim

ACKNOWLEDGMENTS

Qian Liu

Fatma Lotfy

Shahira Loza Doss

Wendy Luhabe

Ana Maria Magni Coelho

Mwamvita Makamba

Nabila Marcos

Estefany Marte

Rosa Maria Marte

Daniela Martin

Tebogo Mashego

Parul Mittal

Manar Al-Moneef

Vania Neves

Chebet Ng'ok

Celeste North

Violeta Noya

Angela Oduor

Sasha Olenina

Renata Pessoa

Sandra Portugal

Melek Pulatkonak

Yeshasvini Ramaswamy

Leila Rezaiguia

Xiomara Ricardo

Ana Sanchez

Sam Shiraishi

Lyubov Simonova

Lucila Suarez Battan

Dora Szwarc Hamaoui

Reham Thawabi

Silvia Torres Carbonell

Ritu Uberoy

Funmilayo Victor-Okigbo

Alena Vladimirskaya

Crystal Yi Wang

Michelle Wang

Zhen Trudy Wang

IF YOU'D LIKE MORE

CONNECT WITH THE WAY WOMEN WORK

Thank you for reading *Undeterred*. I hope you feel more prepared, focused, and determined to accelerate your success. Visit TheWayWomenWork.com, where you'll find:

- Stories of businesswomen in growth economies.
- Tips, tools, and strategies.
- Career guidance from me.
- A complimentary monthly newsletter.
- Our blog. Note that we accept guest post submissions. Let us know if you'd like share the story of your work experience to help other women in growth economies.

ORDER THE *UNDETERRED* COMPANION WORKBOOK AND ADDITIONAL COPIES OF *UNDETERRED*

I Am Undeterred is a companion workbook for readers of *Undeterred*. It includes the complete set of self-reflection and action exercises to help you practice the six success habits of women in emerging economies. For more information, go to: TheWayWomenWork.com/workbook.

To order copies of *Undeterred* go to TheWayWomenWork. com/undeterred. Bulk order discounts are available to universities, schools, organizations, and other institutions.

HIRE ME TO SPEAK FOR YOUR COMPANY OR EVENT

If you'd like to have me come speak, you can reach me at RaniaAnderson.com.

SOCIAL MEDIA

I invite you to connect with me on social networks.
- *Twitter:* http://twitter.com/thewaywomenwork
- *Facebook:* https://www.facebook.com/ TheWayWomenWork
- *Pinterest:* http://www.pinterest.com/thewaywomenwork

I'd love to hear from you. Share your thoughts about what has inspired you in your career or business, and what you've learned from reading the book. Don't be shy! Go ahead and show me, take a photo of yourself with *Undeterred* or the companion workbook, *I Am Undeterred*, and post it on your social networks. Use the hashtag #IAMundeterred. Or just reach out to me by sending a message using the hashtag #IAMundeterred.

RECOMMENDED READING

For more information on key concepts I refer to in *Undeterred*, I recommend the following five of my favorite books.

The Power of Habit by Charles Duhigg (New York: Random House, 2012).

Switch: How to Change Things When Change Is Hard by Chip Heath and Dan Heath (New York: Broadway Books, 2010).

Outliers: The Story of Success by Malcolm Gladwell (New York: Little, Brown and Company, 2008).

Forget a Mentor, Find a Sponsor: The New Way to Fast-Track Your Career by Sylvia Hewlett (Boston, MA.: Harvard Business School Publishing, 2013).

Executive Presence: The Missing Link Between Merit and Success by Sylvia Hewlett (New York: HarperCollins Publishers, 2014).

NOTES

INTRODUCTION

Epigraph. Lael Brainard, "Political Leaders Often Overlook the Key to Economic Growth: Women," *Guardian* (July 31, 2013). Available at: http://www.theguardian.com/commentisfree/2013/jul/31/political-economic-equality-for-women

1. José Ángel Gurría, cited in DeAnne Aguirre, Leila Hoteit, Christine Rupp, and Karim Sabbagh, "Empowering the Third Billion: Women and the World of Work in 2012," Strategy& (October 15, 2012). Available at: http://www.strategyand.pwc.com/global/home/what-we-think/reports-white-papers/article-display/empowering-third-billion-women-world

GET READY

HABIT 1: BE UNDETERRED

Epigraph. Christian D. Larson (1874–1962) was an American new thought leader and teacher, as well as a prolific author. He developed the Optimist Creed. Source: http://www.goodreads.com/quotes/210975-believe-in-yourself-and-all-that-you-are-know-that

CHAPTER 1: CLEAR

Epigraph. Shahira Fahmy, founder of Shahira H. Fahmy Associates. Website: http://www.sfahmy.com

1. Gender and Development Unit, "Gender at Work: A Companion to the World Development Report on Jobs," World Bank Group (2013). Available at: http://www.worldbank.org/content/dam/Worldbank/document/Gender/GenderAtWork_web.pdf

2. BI-ME Staff, "Saudi Businesswomen Call for New Rules," BusinessIntelligence Middle East.com (October 17, 2014). Available at: http://www.bi-me.com/main.php?id=32885&t=1&c=35&cg=4&mset=1011

3. "China Confronts Workforce Drop with Retirement-Age Delay," *Bloomberg News* (December 25, 2013). Available at: http://www.bloomberg.com/news/2013-12-24/china-confronts-workforce-drop-with-retirement-age-delay.html

4. Suzanne Locke, "A Glowing Future for the Saudi Working Woman," *Yahoo! News Maktoob* (April 29, 2013). Available at: https://en-maktoob.news.yahoo.com/a-glowing-future-for-the-saudi-working-woman-080730180.html

5. Conor Friedersdorf, "Why PepsiCo CEO Indra K. Nooyi Can't Have It All," *Atlantic* (July 1, 2014). Available at: http://www.theatlantic.com/business/archive/2014/07/why-pepsico-ceo-indra-k-nooyi-cant-have-it-all/373750

6. Shanoor Seervai, "India Has Millions of Female Entrepreneurs and They Need Easier Access to Money," *India Real Time* (March 13, 2014). Available at: http://blogs.wsj.com/indiarealtime/2014/03/13/india-has-millions-of-female-entrepreneurs-and-they-need-easier-access-to-money

7. Debbie Budlender, "Gender Equality and Social Dialogue in South Africa," Industrial and Employment Relations Department and Bureau for Gender Equality, International Labour Office (January 2011). Available at: http://www.ilo.org/wcmsp5/groups/public/---dgreports/---gender/documents/publication/wcms_150430.pdf

8. Nithya Raman, as cited by Aparna V. Singh, "Is Gender Bias an Issue?" Women's Web. Available at: http://www.womensweb.in/articles/womens-safety-in-india

9. Ian Mackinnon, "Breast Milk Couriers Help Working Women in Indonesia," *Telegraph* (January 18, 2012). Available at: http://www.telegraph.co.uk/news/worldnews/asia/indonesia/9022565/Breast-milk-couriers-help-working-mothers-in-Indonesia.html

HABIT 2: PREPARE

1. DeAnne Aguirre, Leila Hoteit, Christine Rupp, and Karim Sabbagh, "Empowering the Third Billion: Women and the World of Work in 2012," Strategy& (October 15, 2012): p. 18. Available at: http://www.

strategyand.pwc.com/global/home/what-we-think/
reports-white-papers/article-display/empowering-third-
billion-women-world

2. Malcolm Gladwell, *Outliers: The Story of Success* (New York: Little, Brown and Company, 2008): p. 40.

CHAPTER 2: CONFIDENCE

Epigraph. Katty Kay and Claire Shipman, "The Confidence Gap," *Atlantic* (April 14, 2014). Available at: http://www.theatlantic.com/features/archive/2014/04/the-confidence-gap/359815

1. Bank Audi is a Lebanese Bank that owns Bank Audi of Egypt. According to a Bank Audi of Egypt Balance Sheet dated June 30, 2014, the bank's total assets as of that date were 22,649,771,327 Egyptian pounds. Source (accessed October 17, 2014): http://www.banqueaudi.com/InvestorRelations/Documents/Material%20Subsidiaries/Summary%20of%20BAEGY%20FS%20-%20June%2030,%202014.pdf

2. Donna J. Kelley, Candida G. Brush, Patricia G. Greene, Yana Litovsky, and Global Entrepreneurship Research Association (GERA), "Global Entrepreneurship Monitor 2012: Women's Report," Global Entrepreneurship Monitor Project (2013). Available at: http://www.gemconsortium.org/docs/download/2825

3. Ibid.

4. Ibid.

5. Ibid.
6. Ibid.

CHAPTER 3: COURAGE

1. "Unleashing the Power of Women Entrepreneurs: Women in the Workplace," EY (accessed September 16, 2014). Available at: http://www.ey.com/GL/en/Industries/Government---Public-Sector/Women-in-the-workplace---Unleashing-the-power-of-women-entrepreneurs

2. Catherine Clifford, "Lack of Confidence, Fear of Failure Hold Women Back from Being Entrepreneurs," *Entrepreneur* (July 31, 2013). Available at: http://www.entrepreneur.com/article/227631#ixzz2bx1SJ7Q8

3. Ibid.
4. Ibid.
5. Ibid.
6. Ibid.
7. Marianne Williamson, *A Return to Love: Reflections on the Principles of "A Course in Miracles"* (New York: HarperCollins Publishers, 1992): p. 190.

CHAPTER 4: COMPETENCE

Epigraph. Funmilayo Victor-Okigbo, CEO and Production Designer, No Surprises Events. Website: http://nosurprisesevents.com/team/funmi-victor-okigbo

1. A conclusion reached from the synthesis of research studies, including an International Monetary Fund report prepared by Katrin Elborgh-Woytek, Monique Newiak, Kalpana Kochhar, Stefania Fabrizio, Kangni Kpodar, Philippe Wingender, Benedict Clements, and Gerd Schwartz, "Women, Work, and the Economy: Macroeconomic Gains from Gender Equity" IMF Strategy, Policy, and Review Department and Fiscal Affairs Department (September 2013). Available at http://www.imf.org/external/pubs/ft/sdn/2013/sdn1310.pdf

2. Dean Karemara, "Rwanda: Women Entrepreneurs Share Business Tips from Turkey," All Africa (posted March 27, 2014). Available at: http://allafrica.com/stories/201403270098.html?viewall=1 March 27, 2014

GET SET

HABIT 3: FOCUS

1. Charles Duhigg, "Chapter 1: The Habit Loop," *The Power of Habit: Why We Do What We Do in Life and Business* (Random House, 2014).

CHAPTER 5: CHOOSE

1. From a speech, "Happiness in the Key of F Major," given by Tala Badri at TEDxDubai 2010, YouTube (posted February 10, 2011). Available at: http://youtu.be/zyR1T15yl58

CHAPTER 6: CREATE

1. Aparna Vedapuri Singh, with inputs from Sumedha Jalote, "Young Women in India: Building Careers," WomensWeb.in (posted April 2, 2013). Available at: http://www.womensweb.in/articles/young-indian-women-career

2. Divine Ndhlukula, cited in Mfonobong Nsehe, "Africa's Most Successful Women: Divine Ndhlukula," *Forbes* (posted January 20, 2012). Available at: http://www.forbes.com/sites/mfonobongnsehe/2012/01/20/africas-most-successful-women-divine-ndhlukula

3. Chris V. Nicholson, "DEALBOOK: In Mideast Finance, Women Are Breaking Down Barriers," *New York Times* (June 28, 2011). Available at: http://query.nytimes.com/gst/fullpage.html?res=9506E3DE1231F93BA15755C0A9679D8B63

HABIT 4: INTEGRATE

Epigraph. Nubia Correia: https://www.linkedin.com/pub/nubia-correia/0/a37/953

1. "Business Leadership: Uncovering Modern Trends," Grant Thornton (accessed September 16, 2014). Available at: http://www.internationalbusinessreport.com/Reports/2014/Leadership_2014.asp. Also "Women in Leadership: Style Linked to Emerging Markets," Grant Thornton (posted February 24, 2014). Available

at: http://www.internationalbusinessreport.com/Press-room/2014/Business_leadership.asp

2. Ibid.

CHAPTER 7: CUSTOMIZE

Epigraph. Gordana Frgačić: https://www.linkedin.com/in/gordanafrgacic

1. Georgia Institute of Technology 172nd Commencement Address by Brian G. Dyson, then-president and CEO of Coca-Cola Enterprises, given on September 6, 1996. Available at: http://www.bcbusiness.ca/lifestyle/bryan-dysons-30-second-speech

GO

HABIT 5: ACCELERATE

Epigraph. Marshall Goldsmith. *What Got You Here Won't Get You There: How Successful People Become Even More Successful!* New York: Hyperion, 2007.

1. Ibid.

CHAPTER 8: CONTRIBUTE

1. Nancy M. Carter and Christine Silva, "The Myth of the Ideal Worker: Does Doing All the Right Things Really get Women Ahead?" Catalyst (October 1, 2011). Available at: http://catalyst.org/knowledge/myth-ideal-worker-does-doing-all-right-things-really-get-women-ahead

CHAPTER 9: CONNECT

Epigraph. Lyubov Simonova: https://www.linkedin.com/pub/lyubov-simonova-emelyanova/a/101/863

1. Charlotte Vangsgaard and Filip Lau, "How to Get Ahead as a Businesswoman: Order a Whiskey," *Quartz* (July 21, 2014). Available at: http://qz.com/235944/how-to-get-ahead-as-a-businesswoman-order-a-whiskey-on-the-rocks/

2. Multilateral Investment Fund (MIF), "WEGrow: Unlocking the Growth Potential of Women Entrepreneurs in Latin America and the Caribbean," EY (March 2014). Available at: http://services.iadb.org/mifdoc/website/publications/98704705-c7cc-416c-b103-7797dac0844a.pdf

HABIT 6: LEAD

1. "Business Leadership: Uncovering Modern Trends," Grant Thornton (accessed September 8, 2014). Available at: http://www.internationalbusinessreport.com/Reports/2014/Leadership_2014.asp. Also "Women in Leadership: Style Linked to Emerging Markets," Grant Thornton (posted February 24, 2014). Available at: http://www.internationalbusinessreport.com/Pressroom/2014/Business_leadership.asp

2. Ibid.

CHAPTER 10: CHANGE

1. James Kouzes and Barry Posner, *The Leadership Challenge*. San Francisco, CA.: Jossey-Bass, 1987: p xxi.

2. Divine Ndhlukula, cited in Mfonobong Nsehe, "Africa's Most Successful Women: Divine Ndhlukula," Forbes (January 20, 2012). Available at: http://www.forbes.com/sites/mfonobongnsehe/2012/01/20/africas-most-successful-women-divine-ndhlukula

3. Marcus Buckingham, *The One Thing You Need to Know: ... About Great Managing, Great Leading, and Sustained Individual Success* (New York: Free Press, 2005): p. 8.

INDEX

ABOUT THE AUTHOR

RANIA **HABIBY ANDERSON**, FOUNDER OF TheWayWomenWork.com, is a leading expert on the professional advancement of businesswomen in developing and emerging economies and an executive coach.

Originally from the Middle East, Rania has lived and traveled all over the developing world. Her early career success was at Bank of America, where she progressed to a senior leadership role. She left the bank in 1997 to start an executive coaching and consulting business. For the past seventeen years, Rania has coached businesswomen and businessmen around the world.

Fueled by a deep belief that women are the key to global economic prosperity and a lifelong desire to eradicate gender inequality and help women thrive, in 2010, Rania founded The Way Women Work, an online career advice platform visited daily by hundreds of women from around the world.

Rania is a global speaker, cofounder of a women's angel investor network, a devoted mentor, and a contributor to business publications. She holds a master's degree in Foreign Service with an honors concentration in international business from Georgetown University and a bachelor's degree with a major in business from Oklahoma State University.